THE AMERICANIZATION OF A CONGREGATION

The Historical Series of the Reformed Church in America

No. 26

The Americanization of a Congregation

Elton J. Bruins

SECOND EDITION

William B. Eerdmans Publishing Company
Grand Rapids, Michigan

255 Jefferson Ave. S.E., Grand Rapids, Michigan 49503

Printed in the United States of America

00 99 98 97 96 95 7 6 5 4 3 2 1

ISBN 0-8028-4144-5

To
Elaine
Daniel and Mary
David and Elizabeth
James, Katherine, and Thomas

The Historical Series of the Reformed Church in America

This series has been inaugurated by the General Synod of the Reformed Church in America, acting through its Commission on History, for the purpose of encouraging historical research and providing a medium wherein this knowledge may be shared with the academic community and with the members of the denomination in order that a knowledge of the past may contribute to right action in the present.

Contents

Illustrations

Editor's Preface, First Edition

The Americanization of a Congregation was commissioned by the Third Reformed Church of Holland, Michigan, as a part of its centennial year program. Wishing to do more than the all too common collection of pictures of people in the organizations of the church in its one hundredth year, Third Church solicited the services of Dr. Elton J. Bruins to write the history of the congregation. To his task Dr. Bruins brought professional training as a historian, a familiarity with the archival collections of the Dutch-American Historical Commission, and the desire to make a thorough perusal of all extant records of the Third Reformed Church. Dr. Bruins's vocation as a professor at Hope College, his residence in Holland, and membership at Third Church has been combined with his rigorous research and historical sensitivity to make this an outstanding history.

It is to be hoped that the appearance of this volume will stimulate other churches to do serious studies of their own congregations. All too often church histories are merely local chronicles, or a collection of historical anecdotes more or less isolated from one another, with little sense of the continuity of forces within the congregation, let alone an awareness of external forces exerting themselves on the church. *The Americanization of a Congregation*, by virtue of its careful attention to the continuity of congregational life, as well as an assiduous concern for the greater context of community, denomination, and nation, results in a volume of historical, rather than merely antiquarian, interest and as such can contribute not only to the understanding of this congregation, but to others as well.

In the process of research, it became ever more apparent that the account of the development of Third Church was the account of the Americanization of a congregation. The differences that mark off Third Church from other Dutch churches of the community appear to be largely a matter of the degree of Americanization. In the history of Third Church, almost every Dutch church in the Midwest, and many of the nineteenth century immigrant churches of the East, will be able to find much of their own story. This parallelism of development is such that almost any congregation can measure its own rate of Americanization by comparing its present stance to that of Third. In the relationship of Third Church (actually the second Dutch church) to other Dutch churches of Holland, many another community will see a reflection of the relationship between their own churches.

Because of the degree to which this account of the development of the Third Reformed Church is in part the story of every nineteenth century immigrant church, the Commission on History of the Reformed Church in America made the decision to include this volume within The Historical Series of the Reformed Church in America. While the appendices in particular will be primarily of interest to the members of the congregation, the volume deserves a place in this historical series of the denomination in that *The Americanization of a Congregation* is in part the story of almost half of our Reformed churches.

As such, it is to be hoped that this volume will contribute to a better self understanding within the churches of the Midwest, and a renewed appreciation of the problems attendant upon Americanization by our churches in the East which had completed a transition of being first Dutch, then English, and then American, all more than a half century before the process even began for the churches of the Midwest.

Donald J. Bruggink
Western Theological Seminary
Holland, Michigan

Editor's Preface, Second Edition

Elton J. Bruins undertook the task of a centennial history of the Third Reformed Church of Holland, Michigan, with remarkable qualifications as member, archivist, historian, and educator. Since that time Dr. Bruins has continued a notable career, not only as a professor in the Department of Religion at Hope College but also as head of that department, as academic dean, and as acting provost. In addition to teaching the history of the church, he has served on the Historical Commission of the Reformed Church in America, and is now the director of the A. C. Van Raalte Institute for Historical Studies at Hope College.

However, undoubtedly the most difficult assignment undertaken by Dr. Bruins has been bringing the history of Third Church up to its 125th year. The task has been fraught with danger because with several hundred members, there are several hundred opinions as to what happened during that quarter century. All history is selective, but in this instance there are several hundred opinions as to what should have been selected. Dr. Bruins has been most gracious and open in distributing drafts among many members. Nonetheless, decisions as to how the evidence should be interpreted ultimately have been his responsibility.

Elton is a meticulous historian whose facts can be depended upon to be precise. This gives him a great advantage over those historians who fudge the facts to suit their hypotheses. However, even with impeccable accuracy with reference to hard facts, there are still opportunities for endless debate as to the interpretation and implication of those facts.

One of the hypotheses that made the first edition of *The Americanization of a Congregation* so valuable was that it organized the history of Third Church around the theme of its Americanization—the transition from being a Dutch church to an American church. As the concept was used, Americanization consisted primarily in the transition to English as the language of worship as well as in the use of many forms of American church life such as the inclusion of the Sunday school, the choir, church picnics, and the like.

At the conclusion of his book, Dr. Bruins raises the question as to whether the theme of Americanization remains serviceable. This question is especially important when one considers those who analyze contemporary American culture as theologically inchoate, materialistic, narcissistic, and self-indulgent. Commentators on the American church often see these same qualities manifested in entertainment evangelism and worship. For example, authors as diverse Robert Webber (evangelical), Thomas Day (Roman Catholic), Marva J. Dawn (Lutheran), and John Bell (Church of Scotland) all see much of contemporary religious song as switching the subject of praise from God to the self or the congregation. All see the movement to "praise leaders" and amplified music as destructive of congregational singing. In view of Third's commitment to biblical preaching in witnessing to God, and the worship of God, rather than the entertainment of the congregation, one must raise the question as to whether Americanization continues as a viable goal for Christians in the next quarter century. Is the church to be acculturated or is it to be a culture-transforming agent? It would be simplistic to imagine that American acculturation was only supportive of the gospel in the first hundred years of this congregation's life and only detrimental in the beginning of its second century, or perhaps only as it goes into the second quarter of that second century. Good and evil are never so discreetly separated. However, the cultural context in which we live requires that, in this as in every age, the church assess the ethos of that culture and compare it with the gospel and then seek to be true to the gospel of our Lord Jesus Christ.

Dr. Elton Bruins has done the members of Third Church as well as the larger church an immeasurable service in chronicling the history of this congregation. The purpose of this history, as that of the other volumes in this series, is that "a knowledge of the past may contribute to right action in the present."

Donald J. Bruggink
General Editor

Foreword to the First Edition

Our ancestors who founded our churches, our schools, and our institutions of government provided us with a rich endowment. Mindful of the devotion and sacrifice of their forebears, the members and consistory of the Third Reformed Church in Holland Michigan, determined to memorialize the contribution of these noble people who left this rich spiritual and educational legacy. To do this, it seemed fitting to plan an appropriate observance in 1967, to mark the centennial of the church's establishment.

The membership authorized the implementation of consistory's plans for a major restoration of the magnificent old sanctuary. The committee named to plan a suitable centennial celebration desired to augment the restoration of the structure. The Michigan Historical Commission responded to this initiative by registering the church as an historic building and site and sanctioned the erection of an official state historical marker summarizing architectural features of the structure and historical highlights of the church's first century.

In each of these projects, a tribute is acknowledged to the men and women who made Third Reformed Church distinctive. Yet, the moving story of these people required another dimension, something which could be shared widely through the printed page. Thus, the committee resolved upon a history in which the contribution of these men and women to their church, community and nation might continue to live.

In the research necessary for such a history, the resources of the Dutch-American Historical Commission proved to be invaluable. The commission, composed of five institutions (Calvin College, Calvin Theological Seminary, Hope College, the Netherlands Museum, and Western Theological Seminary), which have all grown out of the Dutch immigration led by [the Rev. Albertus Christiaan] Van Raalte, have cooperated in the collection and coordinated cataloging of archival materials. This history of Third Church not only makes use of these historical collections, but in addressing itself so explicitly to an area of research within the concern of the Dutch-American Historical Commission, it may also provide a stimulus to the use of the archives in the production of other histories of this period.

The preservation of the past is viewed as important within the state, and the Michigan Historical Commission is empowered by law to preserve official records of the state and local units of government. The commission also seeks to encourage other institutions, groups, and regions in the preservation of their own historical records. Thus, while the Dutch-American Historical Commission can be seen as working in close relation to the concerns of the Michigan Historical Commission in its archival work, Third Reformed Church has attempted to put the preservation of these materials to work by producing a history of a church within the perspective of the Dutch immigration to Michigan, and the development of this church within this new land. In Michigan during the second half of the 19th century, the church was usually the center for the educational, moral, and cultural development of the community. While of interest to the church, this detailed history is also of importance to the wider interests of Michigan history.

To accomplish this complex task, Third Reformed Church invited the Rev. Dr. Elton J. Bruins, associate professor of religion at Hope College, to author the work. Professor Bruins's familiarity with the Reformed Church in America, his intimate knowledge of the archival collections of the member institutions of the Dutch-American Historical Commission, his competence as a historian, and his compassion for people are characteristics contributing to a sensitive interpretation of the human story in the church's first hundred years.

The author depicts vividly the panorama of one church's refinement in the crucible of Americanization. The self-sacrificing devotion of the men and women of Third is manifest by the vision and faith which marked their works. Their Chrisian concern can be seen in their leadership and support of the community, in their devotion to Hope College, and in their zeal for the world-wide mission of the Reformed church.

The Americanization of a Congregation will serve as a ready reference to the achievements and dedication of those who labored in the past and for those who take a creative approach to the present and future. They, too, with zeal and devotion may work creatively to build a spiritual heritage for those who follow.

Willard C. Wichers, President
The Michigan Historical Commission

[Note: After many years of service on the Michigan Historical Commission, Dr. Wichers, a long-time member of Third Church, died May 18, 1991. His contribution to the fields of Michigan and local history are immeasurable. EJB]

Acknowledgements, First Edition

The centennial celebration of the Third Reformed Church, Holland, Michigan, offered the usual opportunity to write a history of the congregation. Mr. Willard C. Wichers, general chairman of the centennial celebration, provided the initial encouragement to have a history written of the church that would be different from the usual histories produced by local churches. He called for a definitive history that also recognized the church's place in the community and in the denomination. The author has attempted to reach the goal set by Mr. Wichers.

The author is greatly indebted to many members and friends of Third Church for information and assistance. Several people granted interviews which added to a better understanding of Third Church. In particular, the late Professor Garrett Vander Borgh, senior elder of the church at the time of his death in May, 1968, was especially enlightening in his comments. The historical committee composed of Lavina Cappon, Mildred W. Schuppert, Adelaide Borgman Veldman, Lillian Van Dyke, Myra Manting Weaver, Clarence Jalving, the Rev. Dr. Bastian Kruithof, and the Rev. Dr. Henry Voogd, under the chairmanship of the Rev. Dr. Donald J. Bruggink, gave particular encouragement to the project and assistance in the gathering of material, in making positive criticisms, and in reading the manuscript. The Rev. Drs. Bastian Kruithof and Lambert Ponstein, colleagues in the Department of Religion at Hope College, provided translations of the Dutch sources.

Several people gave very extensive time and much expertise to the task of writing this history. Crystal Walvoord corrected and typed the manuscript twice. Adelaide Veldman, church secretary, cheerfully accepted the countless interruptions to provide information and assistance. Myra Weaver performed the tedious and time-consuming task of compiling appendices two through eleven. Dr. James Prins, Lillian Van Dyke, the Rev. Dr. Gerrit ten Zythoff, and Dr. Bruggink gave most helpful advice for the improvement of the manuscript. The author's family, who has had to live with the researching and writing of this book for more than two years, willingly cooperated in the venture. The author is also indebted to the members of the Historical Commission of the Reformed church who read the manuscript and made the decision to include it in "The Historical Series of the Reformed Church in America."

Acknowledgements, Second Edition

Just as it seemed appropriate to publish a history of Third Reformed Church following its centennial in 1967, so it is fitting to issue a second edition of Third's history following its one hundred and twenty-fifth anniversary celebration during 1992 and 1993. The first edition of 2,000 copies has been depleted. Since 1967, the centennial year, the congregation has undergone rich and varied experiences. Consequently, the new chapter seven is much lengthier than any of the first six chapters. That is also due to the fact that there is much more documentation available in the church archives, especially since the church's newsletter proved to be a rich source of information on Third Church.

It hardly seems to be appropriate to expend funds on a book when the congregation has undertaken a major building program for the new parish hall addition to the venerable sanctuary. However, Third Church received a generous legacy from the estate of Mildred W. Schuppert, who had been a longtime member of the church and a person interested in its history. Consistory moved that a portion of her legacy be used for the publication of this edition. We honor the memory of Miss Schuppert, therefore, in this new edition of Third's history. She attended the adult class sessions when the author set forth the basic outline of the book in the fall of 1993.

The first six chapters are virtually unchanged from the first edition except for the elimination of a few errors and making the text gender-neutral. Cultural attitudes have changed considerably since 1967. In the appendices of the first edition women's names were listed usually by husband's names only. For this edition I have attempted to obtain as many of the names of women as possible before they married. Several women members of the congregation were very helpful in recovering the names of women for these lists. I am especially indebted to Cornelia Nettinga Neevel and Marie Dalman Van Eerden for their help.

There are two major addition to the appendices. Appendix 22 is a reconstruction of the list of the charter members. Since the first record book of the church burned in the Holland Fire of 1871, it is impossible to recover the original membership list (as explained in the introduction to this appendix). However, at least three-fourths of the names have been recovered and preserved for posterity.

Another new appendix is a chronological list of events from the centennial year of 1967 through the one hundred twenty-fifth anniversary year, September, 1992, through June, 1993. The data in this appendix is valuable because it was not possible to include all of this detail in the narrative of chapter seven. Therefore, if a reader thinks that I omitted crucial information in chapter seven, please refer to this appendix for it.

Writing current or contemporary history (which actually is a contradiction in terms), gave me a difficulty which I did not encounter to any extent in writing the first edition. Many members of Third Church have participated in the life of Third Church since 1967 and can be very good critics of what I have written. Many people have given me helpful feedback. However, our own members have differing points of view on some issues. At the conclusion of the process, I simply had to make some interpretative judgments of my own with which some of the readers did not agree. Members and friends who reviewed chapter seven to whom I express my gratitude are: Jane Armstrong, Delores and Jon Bechtel, Chad Boorsma, Gordon Brewer, Elaine Bruins, Glenn and Phyllis Bruggers, Harvey and Jean Buter, Sue Carlson, David Carothers, Gerald Cox, Donald and Jane Cronkite, Kathryn Davelaar, Alfredo Gonzales, Carol and Lars Granberg, Peter Handy, Etta and John Hesselink, Cindy and Mark Hiskes, Jantina Holleman, Lynn Winkels Japinga, Elaine and Eugene Jekel, Donald Luidens, John Lunn, Beth Marcus, William Moreau, William Reynolds, Evelyn and Roger Rietberg, Harold Ritsema, Karen and Peter Schakel, Steven Stam, Deborah Sterken, Elaine and Elliot Tanis, Donald and Lois Van Lare, Betty Lou and

Dennis Voskuil, and Douglas and Kay Walvoord. All errors in judgment are my own, of course.

I am grateful to the Rev. Dr. Donald J. Bruggink, general editor of the Historical Series of the Reformed Church in America, for his counsel, judgment, and wisdom in guiding me through the process of publishing a second edition of this book and to the members of the Historical Commission of the Reformed Church in America for allowing it to appear again in the Historical Series. Ms. Laurie Baron, copy editor, helped me avoid infelicitous phrases and provided continuity in capitalization and punctuation. I am indebted to Hope College for my being able to work on this second edition while serving as director of the A. C. Van Raalte Institute for Historical Studies. Last of all and most important, my thanks to Elaine for her patience with me when I become engrossed in my historical research.

I
A New Church in the Colony

Where does the story of a church begin? The most obvious answer is that the history of a congregation begins with its organization, and for the Third Reformed Church of Holland, Michigan, this was in 1867. Yet the obvious answer is an unsatisfying one. The people who gathered in the First Reformed Church on the ninth of September to form a new congregation were members of the First Reformed Church. That church had been founded after the Dutch immigrants came to western Michigan and settled on the shores of Black Lake under the leadership of the Reverend Albertus Christiaan Van Raalte in 1847. When in 1867 the minister of First Church, Dominie Van Raalte, considered it advisable to have First Church divide into two congregations, the members who lived west of Central Avenue[1] in the city of Holland were asked to become the nucleus of the new congregation. Therefore, since this new congregation was actually the western half of the congregation of the First Reformed Church, the story of the Third Reformed Church can be said to start with the founding of the First Reformed Church.

One other factor entered the picture, however. The members of the congregation which had been formed in 1867 were not Americans by birth. Many could not speak the English language. They were Dutch immigrants who had come to the United States to seek their livelihoods. In an economic sense, they were no different from the millions of other people who emigrated from Europe to America during the nineteenth century. But, in another sense, they were people with a difference. The word "peculiar" might be applied to them if given a positive, rather than a negative, emphasis. Even as the people of Israel were called a peculiar people in the King James Version of the Bible, the Dutch of Holland, Michigan, were "peculiar." Their peculiarity lay in their strong religious background. They had come to a new country not only to achieve a new way of life for themselves and their families, but also to establish a colony in which they could foster the kind of religious and ecclesiastical life they cherished. Therefore, the people who agreed to form a new congregation in 1867 were Christians who had come from the Netherlands, and even within that Calvinistic nation, from a religious group with a particular viewpoint as to the nature of Christianity and how it should be practiced. This is where the story of the Third Reformed Church really begins.

Secession

A better date for the origin of the Third Reformed Church would be October 14, 1834.[2] At that time, a Dutch Reformed minister in the Netherlands by the name of Hendrik De Cock left the Netherlands Reformed Church and formed a new denomination. He and his followers seceded from the state church with which they had great disagreements. Through a period of years, the Secessionists, as they were called, had developed a growing dissatisfaction with the Dutch Reformed Church. De Cock and his people, who had been influenced by the old Dutch Reformed theologians, the "oude schrijvers," felt that the Dutch Reformed Church of their day was untrue to the Christian faith. The "old writers" such as Voetius (1588-1676) and Borstius (1612-1680) emphasized a deep personal piety to which De Cock and his followers adhered. To the Secessionists deep piety was synonymous with Puritanical conduct. In public worship the Secessionists were opposed to hymnsinging both because it had been commanded by the government and because they preferred to sing the Psalms in their worship services.

There was also another aspect to the matter of secession. Since the Reformed Church was closely allied to the government, a secession was not only a matter of concern to the ecclesiastical authorities but also to the political authorities. The concern of the political authorities was due to the fact that the Secessionists were meeting in unauthorized groups. The

The Rev. Dr. Albertus C. Van Raalte, founder of the City of Holland and donor of the property on which the Third Church sanctuary stands.

Napoleonic Law was still in effect; namely, no public gatherings of more than twenty people were allowed without the permission of the public authorities. In the eyes of the government, De Cock and his people were fomenters of civil disobedience when they refused to obtain permission to congregate. The Reformed Church of the Netherlands opposed the new group because De Cock had been encouraging defections from the parishes in the vicinity of Ulrum where he was minister for the sake of the "Secession." He disregarded the privileges and rights of fellow ministers by baptizing children of other parishes when parents of secessionist persuasion brought their children to him. The Secessionists found themselves in a position which neither the church nor the state would tolerate. Under those conditions, persecution was inevitable. Ministers and lay people were often arrested. Several paid very large fines. Seceders often lost their jobs, and many could not find work if they were suspected of being members of the *Afgeschiedenen*, as they were also called. Yet the secession movement grew. Hendrik P. Scholte, who later founded Pella, Iowa, joined the Secession immediately. When Albertus C. Van Raalte was examined for the ministry by the Reformed Church in 1835, he felt that in good conscience he could not agree to the stipulations for entrance into the state church and instead joined the church of the Secession which his brothers-in-law, Antonie Brummelkamp and Simon Van Velzen, had also joined as ministers.[3]

Emigration

In the next decade the general difficulties of the Secession were compounded by the economic depression that came with the potato famine in 1845 and 1846. This national catastrophe led the Seceders to consider emigration. A few Netherlanders in America had written about that fertile country to their friends. As hunger became increasingly prevalent for many in the Netherlands, America came to be thought of as the land of plenty. After learning of the prosperity of some Netherlanders who had gone to America, Albertus C. Van Raalte and Antonie Brummelkamp thought that emigration was the answer to many of their people's problems. They formed a society to encourage emigration and drew up a constitution for a settlement in America called De Kolonie. The congregations of Seine Bolks, Cornelius Vander Meulen, and Peter Zonne heard their ministers' decision to join Van Raalte, and they also chose to emigrate. Emigration to America began in earnest when the Van Raalte family sailed on the *Southerner*, which left port September 20, 1846.

When the ship docked in New York November 17, after a two-month voyage, the immigrants were met by leaders of the old Dutch Reformed Church in America, a denomination which included descendants of the Dutch who had come to *Nieuw Nederland* more than two centuries earlier. The Rev. Thomas De Witt, a minister of the Collegiate Dutch Reformed Church in Manhattan, welcomed Van Raalte cordially, and in Albany the Rev. Isaac N. Wyckoff, pastor of the Second Reformed Church, formed a society to help the immigrants, calling it the Protestant Evangelical Holland Emigrant Society. With the help of these Dutch Reformed ministers in America, Van Raalte received new encouragement in his venture and continued on his way west. While wintering in Detroit, Van Raalte decided not to go on to Wisconsin as he had originally intended but to consider an area for settlement in western Michigan. Through Theodore Romeyn, an attorney in Detroit and a member of a Dutch Reformed family in the East, Van Raalte was introduced to Judge John R. Kellogg of Allegan County in western Michigan. Judge Kellogg, Van Raalte, and an Indian guide went to investigate an area on the Black River as a possible location for the colony. Isaac Fairbanks had settled there in 1844 and the Rev. George N. Smith was located in the same area while ministering to the residents of the Indian village on the south shore of Black Lake near the eastern shore of Lake Michigan. Early in 1847 Van Raalte decided to found his colony between Mr. Smith's Old Wing Mission and the Indian village on the south shore of Black Lake. With emigration society funds and his own personal capital, Van Raalte purchased several thousand acres of land.

The first band of settlers, led by Van Raalte, reached the colony on February 9, 1847. In March another group arrived, followed in the spring by a sizable group which had come via St. Louis and Chicago. In the beginning the immigrants encountered the worst of hardships in their new country. During the first two years the colony struggled to survive and hoped for little else. The Rev. Andrew B. Taylor, minister of the First Reformed Church in Grand Rapids, wrote:

> There is now and has been for some time, a most painful state of want among these devoted brethren. Their provisions have failed them, and some have been subsisting on bran.[4]

Food was scarce and work difficult. In 1847 the men chopped through the woods and the trail, River Street, became a north-south artery which gave access to Black Lake. Stores and houses appeared along Eighth Street during the autumn of 1847 and the summer of 1848, and by August of that year there were fifty houses in the town. Selling lots raised capital for community needs, but the demands of organizing and forming a new settlement, carving it out of raw forests, became secondary to the health needs of the newly arrived immigrants. The disadvantages of the swamp areas near the lake and river became apparent as the mosquitos thrived and malaria and other fevers swept the colony. Practically no one escaped illness in those first two years, and the rapidly-filled graveyard stood as a mute witness to the hardships of settling in western Michigan.[5]

One of the primary purposes of the immigration had been to obtain religious freedom. Even the extreme hardship and demanding physical needs did not prevent the erection of the colony's church, a log structure, 35 by 60 feet, located next to the cemetery on the east side of town. This was First Reformed Church. With a $1,000 grant from the Collegiate Church of New York City, and under the able leadership of its minister, the Rev. Albertus C. Van Raalte, the growing congregation was able in 1856 to erect "The Pillar Church" on the corner of Ninth Street and College Avenue.[6]

The Pillar Church prior to 1900

The village of Holland, Michigan, became the focal point for many Dutch immigrants who came to western Michigan in the nineteenth century. The Rev. Cornelius Vander Meulen and his congregation settled in the village of Zeeland, which had been established by Jannes Vande Luyster six miles east of Holland. The Rev. Seine Bolks settled in a nearby village called Overisel. Hendrik G. Klein was pastor and founder of the settlement called Graafschap, just south of Holland. Ten miles east of Holland, Martin Ypma settled with his congregation in a village called Vriesland. These congregations formed the nucleus of the Holland Classis, an ecclesiastical organization which bound the Dutch immigrant churches together in formal churchly connection and in fellowship. At the first meeting of the classis on September 27, 1848, Van Raalte was elected the president and the Rev. Cornelius Vander Meulen, the clerk.[7]

Union with the Reformed Church in America

In June of 1849 the Board of Domestic Missions of the old Dutch Reformed Church, the church which had befriended the colonists on their way west, sent the Rev. Isaac N. Wyckoff to survey the needs of the colonists. His sincere interest in the welfare of the new colony led him to invite the newly formed classis to affiliate with the Reformed church in the East. The favorable response of the classis was a momentous decision in the religious life of the Dutch immigrants. The classis minutes of April, 1850, read:

> In consideration of the precious and blessed unity of the church of God, and the clearly declared will of our Saviour that they all should be one; as well as the need which the particular parts of the whole have of one another—especially we, who feel our weakness and insignificance—our hearts thirst for fellowship with the beloved Zion of God.
>
> Since the day that we stepped ashore in this new world, our hearts have been strengthened and encouraged by meeting the people of God. The children of God are all dear to us, living in their respective denominations, but in guiding and caring for the interest of our congregations we find ourselves best at home where we are

> privileged to find our own confessional standards and the fundamental principles of our church government. Thus it was gratifying to us to experience from the other side no narrow exclusiveness, but open, hearty, brotherly love. This awakens in us a definite desire to make manifest our fellowship,and to ask for the hand of brotherly fellowship in return.[8]

The presence of A. C. Van Raalte, representing the Classis of Holland, at the May meeting of the Particular Synod of Albany, New York, of the Reformed Protestant Dutch Church, marked the union of the two bodies, one of them a two-century-old denomination located in New York and New Jersy, the other an infant classis from the West. The former denomination was descended from the Reformed Church in the Netherlands but had not been tainted with the rationalism of the Enlightenment which had gained access to the mother church. The Dutch immigrants in western Michigan saw it as their duty and privilege to unite with the daughter church in America because it "had kept the faith."

This important step made by the Classis of Holland was followed by discontent and disagreement. A few of the immigrants in the classis did not share Van Raalte's vision. The church in Drenthe dramatized its feelings by withdrawing from the Classis of Holland in 1852 and uniting with the Associate Reformed Church, a denomination derived from the Scottish Covenanters. In 1857 the Graafschap church left the classis. These churches believed that it had been a mistake to join the Dutch Reformed Church in America. This church used hymns! The new secessionists had not used hymns in worship in the Netherlands and wished to continue the same practice in America. It was also alleged that ministers in the East failed to preach the catechism regularly and that "house visitation" was not faithfully practiced. In effect, the new seceding congregations felt that the churches in the East had abandoned some of the practices which were held with great respect in the secessionist church in the Netherlands. These seceding immigrant churches had confused the general Americanization of the Reformed church in the East with a departure from the true Reformed faith.

Some members in the churches of the Holland Classis lacked Christian charity. The alleged failures of the Reformed church in the East were used to obscure their own basic divisiveness, which was often confused with true piety. The schismatic temper evident in the 1834 Secession was not lost in the migration to America; it was simply transplanted. In 1865 some members from Van Raalte's church left to form their own congregation nearby and built their church facing the market square.[9] The new congregation allied itself with the "True Reformed Church," formed in 1857. The new denomination remained very small for several years, but it fomented an ecclesiastical viewpoint which served to divide opinions sharply in regard to the direction which the Dutch immigrant churches should take. The Christian Reformed church, as this group eventually called itself, came to represent a sizable number of Dutch immigrants. But Van Raalte and the majority of the colonists believed the union of 1850 had been the right course of action and did not favor the new secessionist activity of 1857.

A New Congregation

In spite of the loss of some members to the "True Reformed Church" in 1865, First Reformed Church under Van Raalte's ministry prospered. By 1867 it had grown to approximately 500 members or 250 families.[10] Although the congregation was not unusually large, Van Raalte found his pastoral duties increasingly burdensome and he urged the formation of a new church. Not only was Van Raalte the pastor of the church, but he was also the leader of the community. His duties involved him not only with religion but also with education—he was moderator of the local school district and had founded the academy, the "Pioneer School," in 1851 which was the precursor of the Holland Academy and later, Hope College. Added to work in religion and education were his many financial and business responsibilities, both in his public leadership and his private affairs. With these burdens it is hardly to be wondered at that in order to encourage the division of his church into two congregations, he announced to his congregation in July, 1867, his decision to resign as their pastor. Van Raalte obviously hoped that his resignation would hasten the formation of a new church.

Dominie Van Raalte spurred interest in the new church by offering four lots in the western part of town as a building site. Isaac Cappon and Jacob Labots canvassed the congregation to enlist interest in the new project, and Van Raalte circulated a subscription list for financial support. At a congregational meeting of the First Reformed Church on September 2, 1867, it was resolved that all of the church's membership west of Central Avenue (then called Market Street) should join the new church. The organization of the new church was effected on September 9, at which time two hundred sixty-seven men, women, and children, of which fifty-five men and forty-two women were communicant menbers, became the new congregation.[11]

The new congregation took the name of Third Reformed Church since a second Reformed church (Hope Church) had already been formed in 1862. That church was, however, a small and struggling congregation composed mainly of Hope Academy and College faculty who had been recruited in the East. This second church was true to the Dutch Reformed faith but its services were in English. The Dutch-speaking members of First Church were certainly not ready for that innovation, so there was no inclination for members of First Church to affiliate with the second church. At least the prosaic name of "Third" indicated some courtesy on the part of the new congregation on the west side toward their fellow Christians in Hope Church, a courtesy which was often lacking in the ecclesiastical affairs of the colony.

The major reason for the organization of the Third Reformed Church is given in the introduction to the second minute book of the consistory.[12] It stated that the purpose of organizing a new church was to make a greater impact in the town by having two Reformed church-immigrant congregations instead of one large one. The introductory essay in the minute book said that it was desirous "that there be a multiplying of radiant centers that will send the light of the Gospel into all the surrounding territory, influencing the moral and religious life of all the people."[13] This was the official reason for the organization of Third Church, but there may have been another reason which was not stated.

Although the city of Holland was composed primarily of citizens of Dutch descent, there were Americans who also began to organize churches. Isaac Fairbanks, an early resident of the area prior to the coming of the Dutch, was instrumental in establishing the Methodist Church in 1861.[14] Hope Church had been founded in 1862. The Episcopalians were in the process of forming a congregation in 1867.[15] It seems that Van Raalte was perceptive enought to see that American church life meant a proliferation of churches for good or ill. The Reformed church was clearly the dominant church in the community, but would it remain so if more and more non-Reformed churches came into the colony? It seems reasonable to think that Van Raalte may have urged the founding of a new immigrant congregation in order to meet the "competition." Whether or not this line of thinking had influenced the organization of Third Church, a new congregation would decidedly enlarge the sphere of Reformed church influence in the town. At the time Third Church was organized, members of First Church also formed the Ebenezer Church on the county line southeast of Holland. Soon "radiant centers" such as Third and Ebenezer would join in welcoming new Dutch immigrants and in encouraging the growth of the Reformed church in Holland, Michigan.

The Rev. Jacob Vander Meulen, minister, 1868-1871.

The new congregation, the Third Reformed Church, began to organize its life immediately, although it remained with First Church until the new church building was completed in February of 1868. At the organizational meeting of the congregation on September 9, 1867, the first consistory was elected with Jacob Labots, Robbertus M. DeBruyn, Eppink Van Zee, and Jan M. Kerkhof as elders, and Frederick Kieft, Derk Te Roller, Isaac Cappon, and Cornelis De Jong as deacons.[16] At a meeting of the congregation on October 25 the members called their first minister, the Rev. Jacob Vander Meulen, a graduate of Rutgers College and New Brunswick Theological Seminary. He was the son of the Rev. Cornelius Vander Meulen, the first minister of Zeeland, Michigan. On Sunday, February 16, 1868, two days after the dedication of the new church building, Vander Meulen was installed as the first minister of the new Third Reformed Church.

Third Church was particularly fortunate in the circumstances that led to its founding. The leading man of the colony, Dr. Albertus C. Van Raalte, favored and encouraged it. Its division from First Church was a happy one; in other cities the founding of a second Dutch-immigrant church was often accompanied by bitterness. A sharing of the assets of First Church enabled the congregation to begin without heavy indebtedness. As far as it can be determined, the division of the membership of First Church along geographical lines was generally followed. Dr. Van Raalte, having resigned his pastorate at First to encourage the formation of the new church and to avoid a quarrel over which church would get him as its minister, made it necessary for both congregations to look for new pastors. Third Church was blessed with fine leadership, particularly in the person of Isaac Cappon. Elected as a deacon of the first consistory and as superintendent of the Sunday school which was formed in the fall of 1868, Cappon became a key man in the new church. Cappon, a partner in a growing tanning business, was elected the first mayor of the town when it was incorporated in 1867.

When the new congregation was founded on September 9, 1867, it was a happy occasion. Dutch-immigrant Christians, who had known hardship in the Netherlands and traveled to a new country, had established a city and founded church according to their religious principles. With the prosperity of the colony and the growth of First Church, a new ecclesiastical venture began with the founding of another Dutch-immigrant church called "Third" which was to expand the sphere of religious influence in a young city.

II
A Decisive Decade

The new congregation which had been formed in such a good spirit was soon to face several disappointments. The first was the resignation of the minister. Because of failing health the Rev. Jacob Vander Meulen resigned after only three years of work. He preached his farewell sermon May 16, 1871. The sustained growth of the congregation under his leadership was halted until he could be replaced. On October 5, 1871, from a trio of possible candidates, the congregation chose to call the Rev. Henry Utterwick, a thirty-year-old minister serving a congregation in Vriesland, Michigan. However, before all the elders could sign the call and officially extend it, disaster struck. On Sunday and Monday, October 8 and 9, 1871, the city of Holland was destroyed by fire.

The Great Fire

Holland was then in its twenty-fifth year, a town of approximately 2,500 residents. In the words of a Holland inhabitant, Gerrit Van Schelven, the city was marked by a "steady and healthy growth of both the agricultural districts and Holland City as its natural market."[1] There were several manufacturing concerns with shipping facilities by both water and rail. Holland was proving to be the center of church life for the DutchAmericans through the young education center of Hope College. Here three Dutch language newspapers were published: *De Hollander*, *De Grondwet*, and

Third Reformed Church, 1868-1871.

De Hope. But in that terrible conflagration, almost the entire city of Holland was destroyed.

The first signs of the city's impending tragedy were evident October 8 when showers of fine ashes sifted over the town from a fire which had begun in wooded tracts southwest of town. The late summer and early fall had been marked by drought, so that when strong winds began to fan the flames, the fire spread rapidly. The first alarm came from the bell of Third Church on Sunday afternoon. Many people attempted to fight the fires but they made little progress because of inadequate water supplies.

> As night came on the the wind increased in force, blowing at so great a rate as to make battling with the flames useless, and the fiery monster was soon monarch of the city.[2]

The huge bark piles of the Cappon and Bertsch tannery north of the church caught fire and when the wind changed to the northwest, it blew burning bark toward the city. When the steeple of Third Church caught fire, all hope of saving Holland was lost. The fire eventually destroyed two-thirds of the city. "Within the short space of two hours, between one and three o'clock of

Monday morning, October 9, 1871, this entire devastation was accomplished."[3] Gerrit Van Schelven also reported that

> The entire territory covered by fire was mowed as clean as with a reaper. There was not a fencepost or a sidewalk plank and hardly the stump of a shade tree left to designate the old lines.[4]

An aged widow lost her life in the conflagration. The financial loss was calculated to be $900,000. Two hundred and ten homes; seventy-five stores, shops, and offices; fifteen manufacturing concerns; five churches; and three hotels were destroyed. Insurance coverage amounted to only $35,000.[5] Not even all of this amount was collected. Some insurance companies went into bankruptcy because the Chicago fire had occurred at the same time.

For Third Church and its members the loss was catastrophic. Several members, such as Isaac Cappon, Jan Binnekant, and Engbertus Vander Veen, local businessmen, were burned out. Many members lost their homes. Along with the Methodist Church and Hope Church, Third Church suffered the full effects of the conflagration in that church and parsonage were destroyed. Yet, Van Raalte called for rebuilding and renewal. On the day after the fire, he said, "With our Dutch tenacity and our American experience, Holland will be rebuilt."[6] A local relief committee was organized immediately. The governor of the state, Henry E. Baldwin, made a tour of Holland to determine its need. The sister Dutch-immigrant community of Pella, Iowa, made a contribution, and from the eastern Reformed churches came a collection of $40,000.[7]

The first question that faced the Third Reformed Church was its very continuance as a separate congregation. Upon the loss of its sanctuary, the congregation immediately resumed joint worship services with the First Reformed Church, since that church and Hope College had escaped destruction. On October 16, however, the consistory voted to extend the call to the Rev. Henry Utterwick, resolving to carry through the congregational action taken October 5. This resolve was backed by the congregation at another meeting October 27. Despite the pressing needs in recovering from the great fire, ecclesiastical matters still received due attention, in accord with the intense religious convictions of the people of the city of Holland. Mr. Labots and Mr. Te Roller went to Vriesland to deliver the call to the young minister, who fortunately said, "I could not but seriously think of accepting it."[8]

Isaac Cappon, 1830-1902.

The Great Storm

When Utterwick began his pastorate January 21, 1872, unusual tasks were added to his responsibilities. He was given the burden of raising money for a new church. Relieved of preaching tasks because of the union services with First Church, he went East to visit his Rutgers College and New Brunswick Seminary classmates in the hope that they would suggest persons of means whom he might interest in the rebuilding project. His work was so successful that when he returned in March, 1872, the congregation voted to begin rebuilding. A building committee under the chairmanship of Isaac Cappon was appointed. By the end of 1872, just one year after the fire, the frame of the new church was in place.

The members of the congregation, who for more than a year had suffered from the fire of October 9, 1871, faced another major disappointment and setback as they began the year 1873. On the night of January 2 a severe wind hit Holland, causing this damage described by the editor of the local paper:

> Wednesday night the wind blew a gale, too strong for the Third Reformed Church, which was found in the morning lying around loose [sic], except the two corner towers which remained standing.[9]

The framework of the new church was ruined and a new beginning had to be made. In view of the general conditions in Holland, the results were disastrous. The congregation was carrying a debt of $2,000 from the fire; now another $2,500 was added to its financial burden.

One solution to the problem would have been to continue to worship with First Church. That course of action was rejected. The congregation was determined to continue its corporate existence and to become completely independent of First Reformed Church. Insistent on having their own church, the people decided to build a "relief" church for temporary use. One of the members of the building committee, Cornelis H. Schols, a former ship builder, sketched a plan for this temporary building, to be constructed of the timbers salvaged from the ruined framework. Some of these salvaged materials were used for constructing a parsonage.[10] The congregation moved into its "glorified barn" on February 16, 1873, just a month and a half after the January disaster. Since no pews were available, all worshipers had to bring their own chairs. Pastor Utterwick, considerably discouraged after the January gale, had said, "I sat a whole day by the fire with my head in my hands."[11] But he was much encouraged with the renewed spirit of his people after they entered into their simple building:

> When the temporary church was built, and later enlarged by the addition of a roomy cross section, our plain place of worship steadily filled with people. What spiritual refreshment we received on the Lord's Day when we gathered for worship and whenever we sat communing about the Lord's Table....Who can estimate the good we got then to our souls?[12]

The generosity of many individuals and church groups in the East and the West enabled the church to begin rebuilding in August, 1873. A total of $9,801.18 was received. An anonymous woman contributed $1,000; Prof. J.

The Rev. Henry Utterwick, minister, 1872-1880.

Van Oosterzee of Utrecht, the Netherlands, sent $189. Others gave property: Dr. Van Raalte gave three city lots, and his daughter and son-in-law, Christine and William Gilmore, who were serving a church in Spring Lake, Illinois, contributed another lot. However, not all the funds for rebuilding came from outside sources. The local congregation, despite its financial straits, raised $3,000, and, on the evening of the dedication of the new building, it received an offering of $1,002.49. The cost of the new building, excluding the steeple, the bell, and the pews, was $10,000. The Rev. John W. Beardslee, a pastor in Constantine, Michigan, loaned the congregation $500 to buy pews.

The earliest photograph of Third Reformed Church. The Grace Episcopal Church which burned in 1887, is at the right. The steeple and bell were added to Third Church in 1891.

The New Church

After fire and storm, a particularly happy congregation planned to dedicate the new church on the evening of November 23, 1874, but a severe storm forced the postponement of the service to November 25. The dedication service was a memorable event. Since it had been announced that part of the ceremony would be in the English language, the editor of the one English language newspaper in town attended the service. Members and friends filled the sanctuary to participate in the lengthy service.

The religious leaders of the community were present: Dr. Van Raalte addressed the congregation in Dutch; the Rev. Abel T. Stewart, pastor of the Hope Reformed Church, and the Rev. Dr. Philip Phelps, president of Hope College, addressed the congregation in English; the minister of the First Reformed Church, the Rev. Roelof Pieters, offered the dedicatory prayer. Several psalms were sung and the Van Lente choir, noted for its musical ability, presented anthems in Dutch and English. Pastor Utterwick gave the statement of the church finances in both languages. The editor of the local paper, Gerrit S. Doesburg, was happy to note that the congregation, in spite of all its difficulties, had grown from 97 members to 195 since 1867 and that the Sunday school had many "scholars." But the most impressive aspect of the whole service to this "outsider" was a fact upon which he could not fail to comment: "...a Japanese student [from Hope College was] seated by the side of a Methodist clergyman, singing psalms in a Dutch Church."[13] This indicated to him some very "progressive characteristics" of Third Church.

Two full columns in the local newspaper gave a complete description of the new church, classified by the architect-builder, John R. Kleyn, as "Norman Gothic":

> The woodwork outside is painted and sanded with a light-grey sand-stone color with trimmings and cornices of a brown sandstone....The windows are of a stained glass including the front and chancel windows. The front window is a triplet 10 x 25 ft....The audience room will seat 700 comfortably. The gallery above the classroom is capable to seat 50 persons with sufficient room left for a large organ....The whole inside is plastered with a sand finish with a view to paint it afterwards in distemper.[14]

The size of the new church—ninety feet in length, fifty- five feet in width, and fifty-four feet in height, with a steeple planned to be 125 feet in height—is witness to the tremendous faith and determination of the congregation at a most trying time in the history of Holland.[15]

Hope College

Not all attention, however, was focused upon the achievement of a new building. In spite of the disaster the community had experienced, the people of Holland wished to show their gratitude to Providence for the outpouring of funds with which they could rebuild. Their gratitude took the form of establishing an endowment fund for the Preparatory Department of Hope College. A goal of $50,000 was set. Third Church supported this "Ebenezer Fund." The church recognized the important place Hope College had in the community and said so in a consistory resolution on August 19, 1872, which read:

> The cause of education has also been taken to heart and has been blessed, so that there are already splendid opportunities for higher and lower instruction. Hope College especially is the fruit of

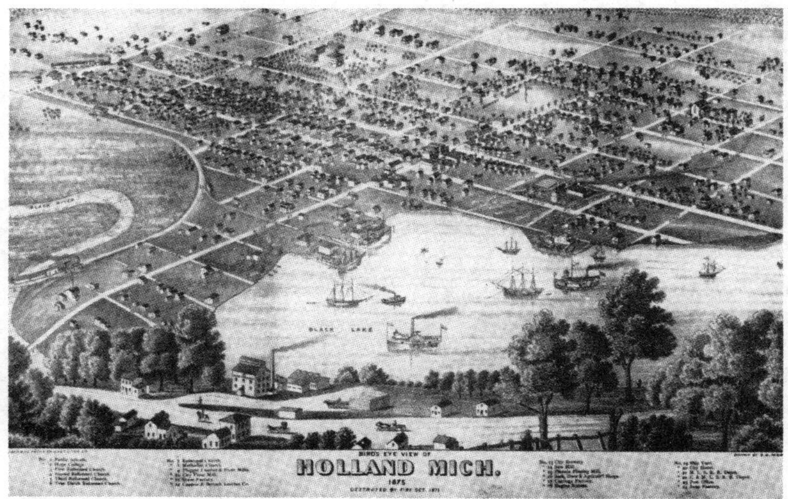

"Bird's Eye View of Holland in 1875" which shows the recovery of the city from the effects of the fire of 1871.

> earnest prayers, of frequent struggles, and generous gifts, and is a blessed fountain out of which has flowed much food for the people of this and other places. Many a youth would not have sought or obtained a higher education had it not been for this institution. Slowly has she grown, and her needs have been multiplied. And as a proof of our thankfulness, and as a monument in commemoration of what God has done for us, we could not do anything better than to help establish a permanent fund....[16]

At a time when Third Church was pressed with its own staggering financial problems, Pastor Utterwick and Elder Kommer Schaddelee headed the local committee and canvassed Holland for funds. Their efforts resulted in $11,000 for the Ebenezer Fund.

Evidence of the "progressive characteristics" of Third Church was not limited to the congregation's vision in rebuilding and in the promotion of higher education through its contribution to the Ebenezer Fund. In other areas of religious and community life, Third Church revealed attitudes which set it apart from the general Dutch-American immigrant community. Primarily under the influence of two people of Third Church the congregation began to Americanize more rapidly than did First Reformed Church and the general community. These two people were the minister, Henry Utterwick, and a leading elder, Isaac Cappon. The roles one or both of these men played in the community in the areas of church music, revivalism, endorsement of public school education, and the temperance movement, encouraged the rapid Americanization on the part of Third Church.

Church Music

In the realm of church music Third Church was unique among the Dutch immigrant churches of Holland. Whereas the latter sang only the Old Testament Psalms in Sunday worship services, Third Church, encouraged by its pastor, Henry Utterwick, sang hymns. It was also through Utterwick's efforts that the Holland Classis, which represented the Reformed church in Holland and the surrounding community, on September 5, 1874,[17] gave official approval to the use of hymns in worship. Van Raalte agreed with this

The Van Lente Choir.

action of the classis but Roelof Pieters, Van Raalte's successor in First Church, did not.

Similarly Third Church was quick to adopt the use of a choir. Frederick J. Van Lente, who was the "voorzanger" at First Church, caused considerable discord there in 1856 because he wished to have a choir assist him in leading the singing of the congregation. He was not given this permission by the consistory, with the result that he organized a private "singing school." Van Lente's choir was so favorably received that it acquired its own building after homes had become too small for rehearsals. This group sang at the dedicatory service of Third Church in November, 1874. Before the congregation moved into its new building, Third Church organized its own choir. Van Lente's efforts had paved the way for acceptance of a church choir in the Third Reformed Church. Not only was Third Church open to music, but having organized its own choir, permission was also given to a community choir to rehearse in the church.[18]

Revivalism

While First Church was reticent to accept the custom of the church choir, it was open to the revivalism which was prominent in American Protestant church life. When Third Church saw a revival developing in 1876, Utterwick and the congregation were completely open to it. The background of the congregation's acceptance of revivalism was the 1866 revival in which many Third Church members had participated while they were still members of First Church. In 1866 a Methodist lay preacher by the name of Clapper had come to the city to promote a revival. Clapper's preaching touched many Holland citizens including some "rough" young people and influential citizens.[19] Since there was considerable response, he outgrew his quarters above a saloon which he used for his revival hall. He then petitioned First Church for the privilege of using its sanctuary, but was denied. His application to Hope Church was also denied. Nevertheless, as Dr. Albertus Pieters wrote in his historical sketch of First Reformed Church, "Van Raalte and the consistory, recognizing this [revival] to be a work of God, granted the use of the church buildings for the meetings." Permission was later withdrawn when Clapper developed certain "Pentecostal" trends, which were considered to be too rabid for Holland's religious tastes. The remarkable thing, however, was that Clapper, "an Arminian, or Remonstrant, and thus an adherent of a theological system to which [the colonists] were bitterly opposed,"[20] was permitted to preach in a Reformed church. Elder Clapper, a Methodist, represented a strain of Protestant theology which had been developed in the Netherlands by Jacobus Arminius but roundly condemned by the Calvinistic Synod of Dort in 1618-19. Van Raalte and his people were strict adherents of the Calvinistic theological system that condemned the Arminian theology which Clapper represented.

Yet, Van Raalte determined to display a tolerant spirit toward the revival. He knew the inherent dangers of revivalism but he saw the good in Clapper's revival and considered it a work of God. Van Raalte said:

> Twenty years I have worked among this people; but where were the fruits? And now, God sends a Methodist to mow where we had sown; and such a Methodist![21]

When a new revival began at Hope College in 1876, it spread to Third Church. For six weeks Utterwick conducted a revival meeting every evening in the church. During that period of time, forty-eight people made confession of faith and united with Third Church, among them Peter Gunst. This hard-bitten Civil War veteran of some twenty campaigns was converted, and he rarely lost an opportunity to let the congregation know what role this spiritual experience had played in his life. American revivalism, of doubtful theological basis from a Reformed theological point of view, was adopted as a perfectly valid means of advancing the kingdom in Holland, Michigan.

Public Education

Alert to American ways and thinking, Utterwick placed his support behind public education, although there was a strong feeling for parochial education or Christian schools in the community. He and Elder Isaac Cappon clearly indicated that they did not favor the colony's original intent to have a system of parochial education. When Van Raalte and Antonie Brummelkamp had drawn up their appeal for support in 1846 "To the Faithful in the United States of America," they said:

> Our hearts' desire and prayer to God is, that in one of those uninhabited regions in America there may be a spot where our people....may find their temporal conditions secured....and we

> would desire that they, settling in the same villages and neighborhoods, may enjoy the privilege of seeing their little ones educated in Christian schools....[22]

Undoubtedly the Pioneer School, the institution founded by Van Raalte, had its origin in that hope. In 1857 First Church established a school for the children of the congregation, even though public education had begun in the community. But this school failed for lack of support.[23] Isaac Cappon supported the public schools, although it is to be understood, according to Henry Lucas, that

> these schools were decidedly Reformed in emphasis of their teaching. Bible reading, singing of hymns and psalms, prayer, and sometimes, after school hours, catechetical instruction, were part of the school activity.[24]

At the first meeting of the new Board of Education, after the reorganization of 1874, Mayor Isaac Cappon was elected the president of the board.[25] He had also served on the board of trustees of the previous system for public education. In September of 1879 when a new school building was dedicated, Henry Utterwick, the speaker for the occasion, said, "Our public schools are to us American citizens a great treasure." In that address he deplored the idea of Christian schools which some Reformed Church in America people wanted and which were fully espoused by the Christian Reformed Church, "as though our public schools were incompatible with or antagonistic to a sound Christian education." He saw no need for parochial schools. Nor did he want Dutch taught in the public schools as was being espoused at that time by Editor Hermanus Doesburg of *De Hollander*.[26] Said Utterwick, "our schools should not be any nationality but English."[27] Utterwick's attitude and Isaac Cappon's actions on behalf of public schools set the mood for the congregation's attitude. Many members of the church through the years have served public education as board members or as teachers.[28] The church never gave much support to the parochial system which, nonetheless, developed eventually in the community.

Temperance

The fourth area in which the Americanizing influence affected Third Church was the temperance movement. This influence came from Isaac

Cappon. His role in advocating temperance is all the more noteworthy in view of the fact that he was also Holland's leading citizen.[29] Like most of the residents of Holland, Michigan, he had been born in the Netherlands. As a youth of eighteen years he came to the colony with his widowed mother in 1848. In 1857, after serving an apprenticeship as a tanner in Grand Rapids, he founded his tannery in Holland in partnership with John Bertsch. During the Civil War his business grew rapidly on the site between Eighth and Ninth Streets and Pine and Maple Avenues, which later became the location of the Holland Civic Center. Although his tannery burned in the fire of 1871, Cappon and Bertsch recouped their losses and rebuilt immediately. Apparently Cappon had both good insurance and substantial financial resources, because after the fire, Cappon was able not only to reestablish his business, but also to build a home at the corner of Ninth Street and Washington Avenue for the regal sum of $10,000. It was one of the finest homes in Holland.[30] The community was extremely proud of the immigrant lad who had built a successful business. This pride also had an element of self-interest in that Cappon's tannery proved to be the mainstay of the city's economy in the 1870s when a general depression followed the national panic of 1873. The editor of the *Holland City News* called his business "mammoth" and the largest in the state of Michigan. "In short, this is the main-stay of the City of Holland, as many a father of a family will gladly testify. Long may they prosper."[31] Cappon's financial success allowed him to travel widely, attending the Paris Exposition in 1878. He was prominent in the affairs of the city, serving four times as mayor of the city and as president of the school board. Third Church benefited from his financial generosity and his leadership in congregational affairs.

But Isaac Cappon, to the dismay of many fellow Hollanders, espoused the cause of temperance. This movement, which was gaining support in American Protestantism, came to Holland by way of the Methodist Church. The Dutch-immigrant churches were by no means the instigators of a movement that in time they supported wholeheartedly. The Dutch were not "total abstainers!" Dominie Van Raalte kept a keg of beer on hand at all times, and the use of beer and liquor among the residents of Holland was not at all uncommon. In 1878 the city supervisor, Gerrit Van Schelven, reported that $900 had been collected in liquor taxes from establishments within the city of Holland. These establishments included five retail liquor dealers, two retail beer dealers, and one beer manufacturer. When the liquor traffic and attendant evils were being considered a national problem, Isaac Cappon backed the cause of temperance in a city that did not abhor alcoholic beverages.

At the organizational meeting of the Holland Temperance Association in the Methodist Church on August 24, 1875, William Cropley presided and Arend Visscher, a member of Third Church and a Holland attorney, was appointed secretary. Isaac Cappon, Professor Charles Scott, a teacher at Hope College and a member of Hope Church, and C. L. Matchan, were appointed to draft the articles of association. This group met regularly and soon became involved in attempts to legislate a greater degree of temperance. Cappon and twenty petitioners asked the City Council to raise the liquor tax fee from $150 to $500. But the "Ways and Means" Committee reported to the City Council saying that a high tax was:

> an indirect measure of abstinence....The large majority of the inhabitants of Holland are sobre [sic] in the use of liquor, and don't need any guardianship. We have mostly been brought up where a moderate use of spiritous beverage is general, and no shame on it, and which [sic] has come customary with us.[32]

Brother Cropley submitted a minority report asking protection from the "evil results" of intoxicating beverages and claimed ninety-two people signed a petition agreeing with his position. When the Women's Temperance Union was founded in Holland, May 12, 1877, Helen,[33] a daughter of Isaac Cappon, was one of the officers. Cappon's efforts were successful. By the turn of the century, the church backed the temperance movement to the fullest extent, and Prohibition was on the way.

These "progressive characteristics" were being demonstrated by the leadership of the church in the decade following the Holland fire. Signs of Americanization and the adoption of new customs were evident, but emerging were two major challenges that were to test Third Church: the anti-Masonry controversy and the adoption of the English language for worship. At the beginning of these bitter struggles, Third Church lost its dynamic young minister, Henry Utterwick, who resigned. He not only left Holland in disgust, he also left the denomination and became the minister of the Second Congregational Church in Grand Rapids, Michigan. He was disappointed in what he thought was slow progress toward Americanization. Little did he realize that he became known as one of the effective pastors in the history of Third Reformed Church. Unknowingly, he had led the congregation to face the fact of inevitable Americanization, which, in the long run, made Third Church a very successful congregation in the city of Holland.

III
Troubled Days

In the latter part of the nineteenth century, Third Church experienced two painful controversies: the conflict over the right of Christians to be members of the Masonic order, and the change from the Dutch to the English language in the worship services. In both controversies, Third Church lost a considerable number of members because of the positions it took. During the controversy over the Masonic question, several members returned to the Pillar Church, which had seceded from the Classis of Holland in 1882. During the change from Dutch to English, many members returned to the First Reformed Church, now located at Ninth Street and Central Avenue. But painful as these two major controversies were, Third Church continued on its progressive course. In the reshuffling of members among the churches at that time, Third Church presented an image in the community that was progressive, American, broadminded, and far in the vanguard of the other Dutch-immigrant churches in the city. It clearly stood out as a church of Reformed persuasion but of American orientation and direction.

Masonry

The conflict over Masonry[1] came to the immediate attention of the Holland community in 1874, when it was heard that First Church had discovered two lodge members in its midst and had threatened to excommunicate them. This threatened action by First Reformed Church might seem astonishing to an American Protestant today. At that time, it was perceived quite differently. Not only had there been anti-Masonic agitation in the United States during the 19th century, but there had also been virulent opposition of the church in Europe to Masonry. The Roman Catholic church had outlawed membership in Masonry. Most Dutch immigrants who had come out of the Secession of 1834 simply assumed that it was impossible for a Christian to be a Mason and for a Mason to be a Christian. Their attitude was perfectly understandable since many lodges in Europe were militantly anti-Christian. Therefore, it was indeed shocking to the congregation of First Church in 1874 to learn that two members had joined a secret society.

In spite of anti-Masonic agitation in America in the nineteenth century, Masonry in America had quite a different understanding and feeling towards the Christian church than in Europe. Many Christians felt church membership and Masonic membership were completely compatible. Although many American Protestants joined lodges, including Reformed Church in America people in the East, the immigrant church members in Holland, Michigan, could not accept this open attitude toward the secret society. They were astounded to learn that even ministers in the Reformed church in the East were members of lodges. These ministers were also on the board of Hope College. One, the Rev. G. Henry Mandeville, even served as the provisional president of the college following the resignation of President Philip Phelps in 1877. Since Hope Reformed Church consisted primarily of easterners, Masons were not uncommon in that congregation, another fact which set that congregation apart from the Dutch-immigrant community.

As early as 1868 the western classes of the Reformed Church in America petitioned the General Synod to clarify its stand on the matter of membership in secret societies. The synod hesitated to make a declaration on the subject because the denominational leaders at that time saw no conflict between Masonry and church membership. This irritated the immigrant churches in the West. Because of the unwillingness of the denomination to rule that Masons could not be members of a congregation, many Dutch immigrants had occasion to vent their spleens against an already mistrusted Reformed church. In addition, the immigrant churches were constantly reminded by the "True" Reformed Church that the Reformed Church in America was virtually apostate anyway. Allowing church members to be Masons was just another sign of apostasy.

When the trouble began to develop at First Church in 1874, Gerrit G. Van Schelven, of immigrant background and one of the articulate and broad-minded citizens of Holland, was editor of the *Holland City News*. In his editorial of May 23, 1874, he attempted to forestall trouble by saying that the issue was not worthy of debate and predicted that following generations would smile about it if it were debated. This remark was followed by very prophetic words:

> we think that this is the beginning of an unpleasant controversy, and may lead to a serious quarrel, and perhaps rupture, within the denomination with which Holland emigration of the past twenty-five years has formally united and identified itself.

Van Schelven tried to minimize the dispute by reminding the community of what the eastern section of the Reformed church had done for the colonists:

> In a special manner they have come to our relief after the great catastrophe of 1871 and again rebuilt our churches; and in various ways better known to these same agitators than to us, they have and are still annually distributing their thousands among the Hollanders in the West, in promoting their religious, educational and material development.

The editor may have been trying to say that if the agitation really erupted the flow of funds from the eastern churches would halt, but he basically agreed with the Reformed Church in America's position that membership in the secret society should be left to the conscience of the individual. He concluded his editorial with a plea for tolerance.

No serious rupture in First Church developed, possibly because of the great influence of Dominie Van Raalte, who was still living at this time, although he was no longer pastor of First Church. Van Raalte was reportedly bitterly opposed to secret societies and Masonry in particular. He was knowledgeable of the movement in so far as literature of his time could produce information on it, as witnessed by some of the books in his library. But Van Raalte was a good Christian and churchman. He did not approve of the excommunication of a Mason from the church unless that person's membership in the lodge caused him to live and act in an un-Christian fashion. "You must have sin, which comes out of free masonry, e.g., a breaking of the moral law. And the Classis will otherwise not give its approval, and at least I will oppose this as long as I can."[2] He refused to agree that Masonry should be considered a test for church membership as the Roman Catholics and Christian Reformed members considered it should be. There was no more public scandal over the question until after Van Raalte's death at the close of 1876.

The presence and problem of secret societies continued to plague the Dutch-immigrant churches. The congregations in Holland were reminded constantly of the "evil" in their midst. The Holland City Lodge No. 192 of the International Order of Odd Fellows held its weekly meetings on Tuesday evenings in their hall. The Unity Lodge No. 191 of the Free and Accepted Masons met in the Masonic Hall on Wednesday evenings. There were enough Americans in the city, not of Dutch descent, to keep the two lodges going. Their social activities were reported regularly in the *Holland City News*.

Reformed church members in the city were disturbed in 1877 when theological education at Hope College was suspended because of a lack of funds. The weekly meetings of the local lodges would seem to have had nothing in common with this event, but in the mind of the immigrant they were connected. The man elected to serve as provisional president of the college until its financial affairs could be cleared up, the Rev. Henry Mandeville, a prominent Reformed church minister in the East, was a Mason. The Dutch-immigrant mind came to this conclusion: Free-masonry was the cause of the suspension of theological education at Hope College![3]

The time was ripe for a full-blown controversy over the matter, and the storm hit in early June, 1879, when Edmond Ronayne, a former Mason and itinerant lecturer, visited the community and for three evenings spoke on the supposed evils of the lodge to large audiences in stately First Church. The new editor of the *Holland City News* commented: "Nothing ever occurred in this city, to our knowledge, that drew together such an immense audience (unless it be Forepaugh's Circus)...."[4] The emotional impact of this lecturer's visit can be seen very clearly in the reaction of Editor Doesburg to what he considered was a scandal. His comments are lengthy but they are unequaled in his expression of disgust over this "religious circus":

> Let us pry into the motive of this commotion. Was it done to keep the Dutch people from joining that society? That would seem useless, for there is no race in existence more prejudiced against it. Was it then to draw Hollanders out of the order? That cannot be; for history of a few months tells us that nearly all of them have withdrawn. At any rate, such a course would not tend to lead anyone away from an association of his own choice, but would rather tend to consolidate them, for action gives reaction, as was shown on Wednesday evening, when the Freemasons had a larger session than for years previous. Was it then to arouse the morbid curiosity of the youth so as to have them join afterwards? This we cannot believe either, the consistory of that church do not believe in anything of that kind.... What then was the object of throwing a bone of contention in the midst of this community? What then was the object of breeding acrimony, quarrels and strife? Is that Christianity? Is that peace on earth and good will to men? No! Most emphatically—No!...We are neither Mason nor a member of the Reformed Church, and can therefore afford to speak out freely; besides it is our duty as a journalist. We don't hesitate to call it a disgrace to the history of this city, and especially to *that church* and we believe firmly that if the spirit of its first pastor could rise and speak, he would say, *to what use is this my temple put*?

The early June meetings had serious consequences. During the month of July reports were coming from First Church that spoke of secession, because a sizable group of members felt that they could no longer be affiliated with the Reformed Church in America. When this came to the ears of Editor Doesburg, he had some unkind words to say. He felt the true motives of the "trouble-makers" at First Church were now clear. They could not "rule" the Reformed Church in America and change its policies in regard to the secret society, so they would now attempt to "ruin" the Reformed church by seceding. This "rule or ruin" policy did not appeal to him and he claimed it would set the "dial of progress...back 25 years in this Colony."[5]

The conflict over Masonry erupted only twelve years after Third's peaceful separation from First Church, and since the churches were so similar in constituency, it was inevitable that Third Church should become involved in the controversy. At the meeting of the consistory of Third Church on August 29, 1879, two months after the Ronayne meetings, Elder Kommer

Schaddelee brought up the matter. He requested the consistory to petition the Holland Classis to declare its attitude on secret societies. In the introduction to the statement he presented, he left no doubt about his feelings on the matter. He remarked pointedly: "The order of Masonry has its foundation in Baal."[6] Schaddelee considered himself to be a spokesman for God in the matter, for he quoted Jeremiah 15:19, "If you utter what is precious and not what is worthless, you shall be as my mouth." More of his "precious" words to the consistory that night were an elaboration of a point that was particularly scandalous to him—that ministers of the Reformed Church in America were members of a lodge. Such men "cannot be office bearers unless they give the right examples themselves," for according to his line of thinking, no Christian, to say nothing of the ministers, could rightfully belong to a lodge.

Schaddelee's petition was put to a vote. There were five "yeas" in support and three "nays,"—Pastor Utterwick, Henry Manting, and Isaac Cappon refusing to support his contentions. In the minutes of the consistory of the church no further reference is made to the question of the secret society. The matter came before the Holland Classis, which petitioned the General Synod in April, 1880, to study the matter again. In June the synod refused to say more about the question and repeated that it was the prerogative of the consistory to deal with the matter. The majority of the churches of the Classis Holland disapproved synod's stand, but accepted the ruling reluctantly.[7]

This controversy was one of the three reasons Utterwick gave in April, 1880, for resigning from Third Church. The classis was thus deprived of his moderate stand in the crisis. In February, 1880, First Church had lost through death its able minister, the Rev. Roelof Pieters, the successor of Van Raalte. During his ministry at First, Pieters' leadership forestalled the secessionist movement. But after his death leaderless First Church, which was unable to find a successor for three years, drifted away from the denomination, and in the early part of 1882, it, as well as several other Reformed churches, seceded from the denomination.

This was a sad and tragic time for the Reformed Church in America in the city of Holland. In a court settlement the secessionist group in the First Reformed Church (which was the majority of the members) was awarded the property of the beautiful Pillar Church. The minority group which did not secede from the denomination but were now without a church building formed the nucleus of the continuing body of the First Reformed Church. When the classis attempted to meet in First Church March 1, 1882, two days after the congregation voted to leave the classis, the doors of stately Pillar Church were closed to it. The classis then adjourned to Third Church "for an orderly meeting."

Although the majority of the congregation of the oldest church in the city left the denomination, Third Church did not secede. A more rapid Americanization process had been taking place in Third, a condition not true at First Church. In the fifteen years from 1867 to 1882 the congregation of Third Church had developed an outlook quite different from its sister congregation. Undoubtedly this difference was due in part to the broad interests of Henry Utterwick and Isaac Cappon. However, Third Church did suffer losses. Kommer Schaddelee, the elder mentioned previously, left with his wife and joined the Pillar Church, which affiliated with the Christian Reformed church in 1884. A small group called the Lake Shore Congregation, the membership of which had been in Third Church and which met for services at Macatawa Park, cut themselves off from Third Church. According to the calculation of Dr. Dubbink, thirty-four members left Third Church over the question of Freemasonry, but according to the statistics reported in the minutes of the General Synod, Third Church lost over 100 (including the Lake Shore group) during the time of controversy. Third Church definitely was involved in the whole controversy, but it chose to stay with the denomination; secession as a course of action was not to be tolerated. When the Pillar Church seceded, leaving only a remnant of its former membership to continue in the new First Church at Ninth and Central, Third Church became the largest and most prominent Reformed church in the city. However, the new First Church recovered quickly, and with Hope Church, soon joined the ranks of the leading congregations in the city of Holland. Because of the secession, the Pillar Church forfeited its place of leadership in religious affairs in Holland, a position it had enjoyed from 1847 to 1882.

English

The explosive nature of the conflict over the Masonry question tended to push another problem into the background: the change from Dutch to

English in the worship services. This change was not completed until 1896, exactly forty-nine years after the colony of Holland was founded. When this fact is so stated, it seems to imply that Third Church was backward in adopting the full use of English. Actually, backwardness was not the case. Instead, Third Church was the most progressive Dutch-immigrant church in the community in this matter. In the words of the Rev. Henry E. Dosker, the immigrants in this Dutch town "worshipped their Dutch and clung to it with a grip of steel...."[8] The community was unlike other Dutch settlements in the cities of western Michigan which contained enclaves of Dutch immigrants. Muskegon, Grand Rapids, and Kalamazoo all drew large numbers of immigrants, but these towns were first of all American cities, primarily composed of English-speaking people. The reverse was true in the colony. It was a Dutch-speaking community that contained a number of English-speaking Americans. There was no mistake about Holland's being a town where Dutch was prominent. In what would be considered a small town today, there were three Dutch language newspapers: *De Hope*, published by Hope College, *De Grondwet*, and *De Hollander.* For the first twenty-five years of its existence, Holland, Michigan, had no English newspaper.

But the change was inevitable and that change would come with some pain, just as it had come painfully to the Dutch in New York and New Jersey a century earlier. Many immigrants, in the words of Dosker, "cherished the false ideal of founding a little Holland in the wilderness."[9] However, there was another group of people in the city of Holland who were characterized differently:

> Here we find the Van Raalte type....These men came to be converted into bona fide Americans. And since the language of the land must be the language of the sanctuary, it was felt that sooner or later the old Dutch worship must be replaced by a new American worship.[10]

The change from Dutch to English in Third Church came from both external and internal forces. There were several external forces at work. The local public school system, though made up almost entirely of Dutch immigrant children, used English. In an effort to preserve the language there were attempts to have some Dutch taught in the public schools, but the children used the English language in the schools even if they could not speak it before they started first grade. There was in the city a nucleus of American people of non-Dutch descent. Isaac Fairbanks, who preceded Van Raalte to the area, became a prominent member of the city and served in many city offices. Hope College brought English-speaking people of Reformed Church in America background from the East to serve on the faculty. Hope Reformed Church had been founded in 1862 by members of the college community in order to have an English-speaking Reformed church. The Rev. Dr. Philip Phelps, president of the college and an ordained clergyman of the Reformed church, served Hope Church (which met on the Hope campus) as its first minister.

Another instrument that fostered the use of English in the community was the *Holland City News*. The decision of S. L. Morris to start this paper was in response to an existing need. In the first issue on February 24, 1872, Morris clearly stated his reasons for beginning an English language newspaper:

> The fact that a city of the commercial importance of Holland, the great Rail Road center of the Michigan Fruit Belt; with her college and schools of learning, her churches, her agricultural and mineral resources, and her facilities for Lake transportation being suppressed from the American reading people for the want of proper expression in the English language, and this want being keenly appreciated by a large portion of our citizens, are sufficient reasons why this enterprise has been undertaken.[11]

The business life of the city also made the change to English inevitable. The use of English by tongues accustomed to a Dutch vocabulary sometimes resulted in a ludicrous mixture of languages. This situation is illustrated by one quotation taken from the consistory minutes of Third Church, January 14, 1880. The minutes read:

> Besloten dat de Com. bij Schaddelee en Cappon om *sidewalk* en *fence* te repareeren aan hunne opdragt her.

When the Dutch words did not come to mind, the clerk of the consistory simply used the English words to express the routine needs for repairs to church property.

The first major force of influence within Third Church to make the change from Dutch to English came from its progressive minister, Henry

Utterwick. Following his graduation from New Brunswick Seminary in 1865, he had served a Dutch-speaking congregation in New York City and then had come back to Michigan to serve the Vriesland church until called to Third in 1871. We can only guess why he wanted to begin English services at Third Church, although he had had his training at Rutgers College and New Brunswick Seminary. But in a letter to Dr. Dubbink, who was then writing his fine brief history of Third Church in 1899, Utterwick said:

> I was called with the understanding that there was to be held one service in the English language as soon as possible. It was as good as a condition of my acceptance, and I labored for it all the time.[12]

Early in his ministry at Third Church, Utterwick conducted three services every Sunday: Dutch services in the morning and in the afternoon, the traditional style for the immigrant churches, and an English service in the evening. His idea was that he would eventually have a Dutch service in the morning and an English service in the evening as the next step. Then those members who wished to attend two Dutch services a Sunday, as was the custom, would attend the Dutch service in the afternoon at First Church. Those members who wished to attend a second service on Sunday but one in English could attend Third in the evening. Opposition to having an English service became so strong that in 1879 Utterwick gave up the idea and also discontinued catechising in English. The conservative forces in the church had won the first round. As has been stated before, the insistence upon Dutch and the growing Masonic controversy caused Utterwick to resign from Third Church. Nevertheless, Utterwick, in pressing for a change, forced the church to face the reality that in time the prevailing language would be English.

Utterwick's sucessor did little to advance a change to English. The Rev. Dirk Broek had an interim kind of ministry during his pastorate at Third Church from 1880 to 1888. Feelings were so high over the Masonic troubles that he chose to do nothing during his ministry to stir the dust of any controversy. There is evidence of attempts to have English services, but apparently nothing was done to further them with the exception of one resolution in the consistory minutes of December 11, 1885, approving union services in English with First Church on alternate Sunday evenings, This resolution was not implemented. Broek's successor, the Rev. Henry E.

Dosker, was able, within his five-year pastorate, to lead the congregation to accept English almost completely.

Dosker was able to effect the change by concentrating upon the needs of the young people. Immediately after his arrival in 1889, he organized the

The Rev. Dirk Broek, minister, 1880-1888.

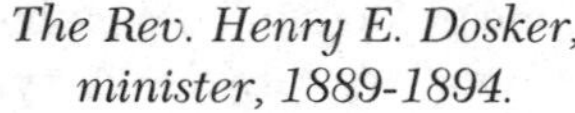

The Rev. Henry E. Dosker, minister, 1889-1894.

The Rev. Dr. Gerrit H. Dubbink minister, 1895-1904.

Young People's Society which later affiliated with the burgeoning Christian youth movement of Christian Endeavor. This thriving organization had been founded in Portland, Maine, by the Rev. Francis E. Clark in 1881, and the new movement swept the country. The young people's group obviously met a need at Third Church, for forty-four youths became members at the time of its organization and there were seventy-two members at the close of its first year. For their first anniversary celebration in 1890, the group held a party to which 350 people came for a "full program" and coffee and cake. It is to be noted that all of these activities and meetings were conducted in English. By this time most of the Sunday school classes were also conducted in the English language.

Under Dosker's leadership, attempts to make the full change began in earnest. Dosker realized the church would lose its young people to Hope Church if it did not change to English. He began by refusing to resort to three preaching services to satisfy the proDutch element in the congregation.[13] Change had to come and he looked for the right psychological time. In 1891 both First and Third "deemed [it] absolutely necessary" to initiate union English meetings.[14] English services were instituted every other week. More importantly, the Sunday school services were changed from the afternoon to the morning, after the worship service. According to Dubbink, "this gave the young people practically two English services during the day, since many went to Hope Church in the evening." But this arrangement had its dangers, for the young people might well stay there! In the fall of 1892 Third Church began to hold English services every Sunday night in its own sanctuary and broke off the connection with First Church. Two years later at a congregational meeting in September, 1894, the membership approved changing the morning service to English and having the Dutch service in the afternoon.

This change in September, 1894, had apparently been conditioned by attempts in August of that year to unite First Church and Third Church into a collegiate-type system. The plan was that First Church would be the Dutch-speaking church and Third the English-speaking congregation. It is interesting to note that First and Third churches still felt a "togetherness" and attempted to effect some kind of arrangement in order to handle the language question. This attempt to have a combined congregation in two church homes failed. No further progress was made by Dosker, because he left in 1894 to become the church history professor at Western Seminary. His successor was as eager for the full use of English as he had been. When the Rev. Gerrit H. Dubbink, fresh out of the seminary in 1895, accepted his call to Third Church, he did so on the basis of being allowed to continue an English service every Sunday morning. Within six months, on January 1, 1896, the church adopted English exclusively for all its services of worship. Dubbink apparently favored this step, but he did not explain how it actually came about. At least the change was made: Third was the first Dutch-immigrant church in Holland to worship God entirely in English.

Dubbink said, however, in his history of Third Church, that the change "was a painful step," as is indicated by the loss of several members.[15] Third's loss proved to be First's gain. The membership record of First Church clearly shows the transfer of several members to its congregation. One member left Third for First in 1894; fourteen members left in 1895; fifteen members went to First Church in 1896, the year the language change was made; seven went in 1897; and one in 1898, thirty-eight members in all. Other members left Third at this time and organized the Fourth Reformed Church a few blocks away. Of the fourteen members who founded this church on March 13, 1896, two months after Third adopted the full use of English, nine were from Third Church. These people "felt that a Holland-speaking church was still a necessity for the west side of the city."[16]

The move of Third Church to the exclusive use of the English language was much in advance of the other Dutch-speaking churches in the city and environs. First Reformed Church began an English service on Sunday mornings in 1906 and continued an afternoon Dutch service until 1923. Most Reformed churches did not make the change to the English language until the decade following World War I. Fourth Reformed Church had made the change by the time the Rev. J. F. Heemstra had left in 1928. The tenacity for the Dutch in Holland, Michigan, was seen in the organization of the Seventh Reformed Church on June 19, 1924. It was a church for the "Dutch only." Eighteen families joined the new organization. But in 1937 it was reported (seemingly as a newly discovered fact) that "younger people do not unite with a Dutch church."[17] After World War II this congregation disbanded. English finally won in the Reformed churches of Holland, Michigan, and Third Church had set the precedent.

In 1923, the Classis of Holland formally recognized the use of English— for ecclesiastical purposes. Then, the classis was merged with the Classis of Michigan[18] of which Hope Reformed Church was a member, and classis boundaries were realigned. Hope Church became ecclesiastically united with the other Reformed churches in Holland, Michigan.

On the negative side, it must be noted that Third's early change to English meant that any new Dutch immigrants were not likely to affiliate with Third Church. But Third was now in a position, along with Hope Church and the Methodist Church, to gain members from the American Protestants who moved to town. Many "new" people began to enter its ranks. This was partly why Third Church greeted the twentieth century with an openness that led to new growth and with a progressive mood in which to conduct its affairs. The ultraconservatives in the church had left the congregation following the two great controversies. Third was free to move ahead, and it did.

IV
To Make Christ Known

The Americanization process at work in the Third Reformed Church is a study in contrasts. After surviving the conflict over Masonry and having made a fairly rapid change from Dutch to English in the worship services, it seemed that the Americanization process was complete, and a Dutch-immigrant congregation had become a fairly typical American Protestant church. But this was not the case. The congregation had Americanized much more rapidly than the other Dutch-immigrant churches in Holland, Michigan. The progressive spirit would continue to mark its outlook; however, the process of Americanization was curiously slow in some areas. During the pastorates of Gerrit H. Dubbink (1895-1904), Evert J. Blekkink (1905-1912), and Martin Flipse (1913-1920), the church was particularly progressive in promoting the world-wide cause of Christian missions. The congregation went to an extreme in its patriotism during the trying period of World War I. At the same time, the church struggled painfully with the matters of Sabbath observance and social practices. It still reflected an extreme caution in these matters. Fortunately, the church's ministerial leadership enabled it to Americanize without having catastrophic conflict engulf the congregation.

The Automobile and the Sabbath

The Rev. Evert J. Blekkink was very skillful in this regard. When he assumed his pastorate in 1905, he brought his automobile with him. He had

The Third Reformed Church as it appeared after the addition of the first parish hall in 1905.

purchased this car in 1903 while serving the Second Reformed Church in Kalamazoo, Michigan. The local paper noted that "the automobile fad has at last broken into ministerial circles." It made news that Mr. Blekkink purchased "a five horse-power gasoline runabout to assist him in fulfilling the duties of his office." The car had been manufactured in Adrian, Michigan, by the Church Manufacturing Company. The paper also noted that Blekkink was a "strong advocate of all up-to-date methods and was thoroughly posted on the current topics of the day."[1] The church should expect an up-to-date man to have such a modern convenience.

After accepting the call to serve Third Church, Blekkink shipped his car to Holland by rail. He used it for his pastoral work in Holland, and many children in the Saturday morning Bible classes had their first automobile rides in the pastor's car. But no matter how useful the car was during the week, Pastor Blekkink did not drive it on Sunday! The church may have come to accept English for worship services, but Holland was unsure at this point whether or not it constituted "work" to drive a car on Sunday. The new pastor brought his progressive methods to his work at Third Church, but he was careful not to precipitate any conflict about the observance of the Lord's Day.

Fourteen years after the beginning of Blekkink's pastorate, there was evidently still some doubt as to the use of the automobile on the Sabbath. The Intermediate Christian Endeavor had for its topic on Sunday, April 13, 1919, "God's Day." For the program Wilma Meyer presented a five-minute talk on "Present Day Tendencies toward Sabbath Breaking," and Lambertus Beeuwkes spoke on the subject, "How to Spend the Sabbath Right." This was followed with a debate on the topic: Resolved that the automobile is a help in church work and not a Sabbath breaker. The young people decided in the affirmative. The automobile was indeed a work of God and could be used for the advancement of Christ's kingdom. The Hollanders made careful tests of the right practices for the Lord's Day, and the automobile finally passed!

Patriotism

In contrast to this extreme caution, the congregation quickly assumed the attitudes of extreme patriotism of American Protestantism during World War I. There had never been any doubt on the part of the Dutch settlers in

The Rev. Dr. Evert J. Blekkink, minister, 1905-1912.

the new world about their loyalty to America. When President William McKinley was assassinated in 1901, the sanctuary of Third Church was draped with bunting and crepe. There were many loyal Republicans in the ranks of the congregation, and apparently there was no hesitation about showing their feelings at the death of a Republican president! Approximately at the beginning of America's participation in World War I, there was a question raised about having flags and bunting in churches. The Rev. Herman Hoeksema, pastor of the Fourteenth Street Christian Reformed Church, disapproved the practice of having the American flag in the church and made his position very clear. As a result many members left that church and joined the new Trinity Reformed Church and Third Church.[2]

Third Reformed Church left no doubt about its feelings in the matter of patriotism. The program for the semicentennial celebration of the church in September, 1917, began with the essay, "A True Christian is a True Patriot." A picture taken of the sanctuary at that time showed the interior of the church filled with flags and bunting. A large flag was stretched across the top of the organ pipes in the front of the church. Bunting was draped in front of the choir loft and across the front of the pulpit. Flags were hung at the top of each major pillar and bunting was placed between the windows. The semicentennial celebration was a fitting occasion to display the loyalty of the congregation to the American cause. In the months that followed, the worshipers were often urged to buy Liberty Bonds. October 21, 1917, was designated "patriotic Sunday," and patriotic duty meant buying a bond. This kind of loyalty and patriotism backed the young people in service who were called the "Representatives in the Fight for Democracy."

The sanctuary draped in mourning for the death of President William McKinley, 1901.

In 1918 the editor of the Sunday bulletin indicated clearly the patriotic duties of the congregation. The notice in the March 31 bulletin was part of the softening-up process for what would follow.

> The great need of the hour is courage. Our nation is at war with a powerful enemy. The Church is at war with a mighty adversary. Tremendous courage is needed for Satan's overthrow.

The conflict had reached the status of a holy war, so the editor did not hesitate to say on April 7:

> The Third Liberty Loan drive is on. It scarcely seems possible that here should be a single family that cannot purchase one of these bonds....These appeals of our Government are a test of our patriotism.

When France's national holiday, Bastille Day, came on July 14, 1918, Third Church celebrated the event. "The pulpit is draped with the American and French flags in commemoration of France's national holiday and this is eminently appropriate as the two republics are fighting side by side with a common aim for a common victory."[3] Having had sixty-nine men and

The sanctuary decorated for the semicentennial celebration, 1917.

women in the military service during the war, the congregation celebrated the cessation of hostilities with a prayer and praise service November 17, 1918. In the same year, a committee of elders was designated to ask three high-school members to refrain from dancing at the public high school. Acceptance of complete Americanization in one area did not preclude conservative attitudes in others.

But, generally speaking, the church continued to reveal American attitudes and practices in personal and religious life. Possibly the resistance to change on the matter of Sabbath practices indicates an attempt to stem a kind of Americanization that was slowly eroding the church life of the congregation. A few remarks by the pastor in the financial report of May 1, 1900, called to the attention of the congregation a matter of concern to him, namely, poor attendance at evening worship.

> The attendance in the morning is very gratifying, indeed. But the American habit of attending church only once a day is not commendable.

In 1913, Pastor Flipse said, "Does the attendance at the evening service seem to be below what it should be, give it a lift."[4] Poor attendance at the evening service was part of the price paid for Americanization. Many people coming into the church during the Blekkink and Flipse pastorates were from other Protestant churches and were not always accustomed or agreeable to church attendance in the evening. Many of the broader attitudes in the church brought new people into the membership, and with them came the attendant problems of keeping the proper image of a respectable church among its peers in a very religiously conservative city.

Missions

But if the church could not shine in all areas of church life, it could shine in one: the promotion and support of the cause of missions. During the Blekkink pastorate in particular, Christian missions became the focal point of the life of the congregation. This cause, which had taken hold early in the life of the churches of the colony and which had been nourished at Third Church by Pastors Dosker and Dubbink, came to full flower in the Blekkink period. Evert Blekkink chose the motto for Third Church: "To Know Him and to Make Him Known," indicating that he intended to make the church a strong promoter and supporter of the mission cause in the denomination. Since the congregation had passed the controversies of the nineteenth century, it could turn its creative energy and interest to something more worthwhile—the cause of Christian missions at home and abroad.

Third Church's interest in missions was part of a larger movement of that time with roots in an earlier day. The mission interest which developed in the Reformed churches of Holland was a result of the union of the Classis of Holland with the Reformed Church in America in 1850. The impressive results of that church merger are easily overlooked. The Reformed churches in Holland learned after their union with the old Reformed Protestant Dutch Church in the East that the Classis of Holland had become associated with a denomination that had already demonstrated outstanding interest in and devotion to the cause of missions, particularly missions abroad. Dr. John Scudder and his wife, Harriet Waterbury Scudder, had left America in 1819 for Asia and had been the founder of the Reformed church mission in Arcot, India. The Rev. David Abeel had spearheaded the founding of the denominations's mission in Amoy, China. The Reformed church had been a pioneer in the cause of foreign missions.

Even though the people of Holland faced major struggles in becoming established in America, the mission spirit of the old Reformed church invaded the life of the colony from the beginning. Before the First Reformed Church of Holland had a permanent home, it designated fifteen percent of its benevolent monies for foreign missions and fifty percent for home missions. The date of this action was November 24, 1851, only four years after the founding of the colony.[5] When the young men of the colony who planned to enter the ministry went to New Brunswick, New Jersey, for their education at Rutgers College and the Theological Seminary of the Reformed church, they came in contact with many young men who chose service in foreign mission work. These young ministers learned first hand of the major efforts the little denomination was putting forth in the cause of bringing the gospel to the world.

The mission zeal of the eastern churches found fertile soil in the piety of the new immigrants in Michigan. The avid interest of the Dutch immigrants came to the point of being visionary. In 1864 a plan was devised to build a ship in the Holland harbor for the exclusive service of the missionary cause. The ship would "carry missionaries and missionary supplies to all parts of the world." With elaborate ceremonies, and with the ecclesiastical leaders of the classis present for the occasion, the keel of the ship was laid on the shore of Black Lake, June 24, 1864.[6] Dr. Van Raalte presided, and the Rev. Dr. Philip Peltz, corresponding secretary of the Board of Foreign Missions, presented to the gathering an address which was immediately translated for the benefit of those who could understand no English. The Rev. John Van Nest Talmage, pioneer mission worker in Amoy, China, also delivered an address. Missionary hymns were sung, and the concluding prayer was offered by Philip Phelps, president of Hope College. This ship never reached the stage of launching and its timbers rotted where they were first laid, but a later missionary ship, the *Morning Star,* was launched and used for missionary service.[7] The mission zeal of the East took root in the West. According to Dr. Aleida Pieters, fifty men and women had gone into missionary service by the time the settlement in Holland was forty years old.[8]

Third Church, of course, was not indifferent to the mission interest that swept Holland. As members of First Church prior to 1867 their interest in missions had been aroused by Dominie Van Raalte, an ardent supporter of the missionary enterprise. In 1872, while Holland was struggling to recover from the great fire, Van Raalte commissioned the Rev. Enne J. and Aleida Vennema Heeren for service in India. Four young men of Third Church, Gerrit J. Kollen, Henry Boers, J. H. Kleinheksel, and Arend Visscher, banded together in 1878 and personally supported a young Indian catechist, Elijah Chinnappa, so that he might get a theological education in Arcot, India.[9] In the following year the Sunday school assumed the support of his brother, Yesu Ratman, so that he might graduate from the Arcot Seminary in 1884.

Third Church's interest in the mission cause was crystallized in 1891 when a daughter of Isaac Cappon, Elizabeth Cappon, became the first candidate from Third Church to enter foreign missionary service. She left Holland in August for Amoy, China, where she served until 1904, when poor health forced her to leave mission service. Anna De Vries Warnshuis and her husband, Livingston, served in China, arriving there at the time of the Boxer Rebellion in 1900. Both of these women had grown up in the Christian Endeavor Society, which had always been keenly interested in missions. The Women's Missionary Society was founded in 1896 to promote missions among the women of the church. During Dubbink's ministry, when the annual Thanksgiving offering for missions was instituted, Third's financial contribution to missions rose considerably.

Elizabeth Cappon, missionary to China, 1891-1904.

Blekkink's strong mission interest enabled him to build on the growing commitment to missions that characterized the community, a commitment shared by Third Church, and to direct it into the leading force of the church's life. His choice of the motto of Third Church at this time gives us a picture of his thought. The motto summarized the spirit of what he wanted Third Church to do: "To Know Him and to Make Him Known." Blekkink wanted the church to know Jesus Christ "as the Son of God, the Redeemer of our Souls, our Example and Teacher, King of our lives and as Master of our destinies." This knowledge of Jesus Christ should propel the congregation to make Christ known "by spreading the Fatherhood of God, by sending the gospel to others, by self-sacrificing service to all men, by obeying the commandments, by acknowledging the power of His resurrection over all who accept Him as Lord." The supporting text of the motto rarely appeared in the bulletin of the church, but the motto itself stuck firmly and was used often. A banner bearing the motto was hung across the organ pipes in the semicentennial celebration of 1917. New banners with the words of the motto on them were made for the 125th anniversary celebration in 1992.

The church sanctuary after redecoration in 1912.

Missions constituted the most prominent aspect of Blekkink's ministry at Third Church. The annual report of 1910 indicates that the church program included the Foreign and Domestic Missionary Societies, the Mission Band for young children, and the Young Ladies' Missionary Society. Christian Endeavor promoted missions as part of its program. In the fall of 1909, a mission conference sponsored by the regional Synod of Chicago was held in Third Church. During the public services of that conference, several returning missionaries were welcomed by the gathering, and farewells were paid to missionaries going to the field, including Harmon V. S. Peeke of Japan, James and Elizabeth G. De Pree Cantine of the Arabian mission, and A. Livingston and Anna De Vries Warnshuis of the Amoy mission. In the fall of 1909 after this conference, the consistory appointed three men, "Brothers John Du Mez, John Pessink, and [John P.] Huyser" to serve as a committee on missions. Women and young people in the church had demonstrated their interest; now the whole church was to be involved. In the following year, Dr. Blekkink was appointed as one of the two delegates of the Reformed Church in America to attend the World Missionary Conference in Edinburgh, Scotland. Third Church was most fortunate to have been represented in this famous gathering which laid the groundwork for the twentieth century ecumenical movement. According to the Rev. Martin Flipse, Blekkink's successor, if missionary enthusiasm was an indication of the church's spiritual life, Third Church was very spiritual!

The strong mission interest in the congregation was stimulated by several other factors which prevailed in the life of Third Church in the period of 1895 to 1920. Many missionaries, such as the the Rev. Samuel and Amy Wilkes Zwemer family, became members of Third Church; they provided a supply of ready speakers. The annual report of the Women's Missionary Society of 1915 stated that several missionaries had addressed the group: the Rev. Willis Hoekje from Japan, Helen Vogelson [Mrs. John] Banninga from India, Anna De Vries Warnshuis from China, Jennie Pieters from Japan, and Amy Zwemer from Egypt. The availability of missionary speakers was further increased by fact that the Rev. William J. Van Kersen, western district secretary of the Board of Foreign Missions, 1910 to 1940, was a member of Third Church.

No doubt because of its opportunities to see and hear so many missionaries—to get direct reports from the mission fields—Third Church readily contributed financial support to missions, although prior to the adoption of the annual Thanksgiving offering to missions, the support had not been significant. The Thanksgiving offerings markedly raised the total annual missionary contributions of the church. According to the statistics assembled by Pastor Martin Flipse and given in his address on "Missions and Third Church" at the semicentennial celebration in 1917, the average yearly giving for missions from 1887 to 1892 was $325; from 1892 to 1897, $455; and from 1897 to 1902, $948. After that, the average yearly amounts exceeded $1,000; in 1906 the Thanksgiving offering was $1,200. From 1907 to 1912, $2,617 was the average amount, and during the Flipse pastorate prior to the celebration in 1917, the average amount was $3,518.

The real significance of these later amounts can be grasped when one compares the total giving of the church with the general costs of maintaining the church. The 1906 offering for missions of $1,200 (collected on Thanksgiving Day) does not seem unusually great until it is realized that the minister's salary for a year was $1,200. The annual report of 1913 offers the interesting comparison of the church expenditures for home needs and its contributions to the cause of missions:

General	$1,316.89
Salaries and current expenses	2,115.83
Collected for new parsonage	1,335.83
Home expenses of the societies	979.87

During the same year the following was contributed for missions:

Benevolences	$388.85
Foreign Missions	1,143.81
Domestic Missions	689.67
For. Missions, the societies	851.64
Dom. Missions, the societies	499.00

For the year 1913 the total amount contributed for parish needs was $5,748.42. Even part of that amount included the capital expense of $1,335.83 contributed for a new parsonage. In that year, $3,572.97, or nearly forty percent of the total budget of the church—$9,321.39—was contributed to missions.

Dr. Blekkink took particular pride in the church's avid interest in missions. In the annual report to the congregation in 1911 he said:

> It is with gratitude to God when we think of the unbroken history of the Third Church; her harmonious life; aggressive spirit; her influence and power in the community; and, through her Foreign and Domestic missionary work, her world-wide activities; China, India, Japan, and Arabia; Dakota, Kentucky, Montana, and others; the names of the men and women in these fields have become

> household words. Some of them were born in this church, others held membership among us, while a much larger number, at different times and during the years of preparation, worshipped with us. We believe that Third Church is only at the beginning of her usefulness.

Then Blekkink, who rarely was given to overstatement, felt it necessary to add:

> We need large churches. Without them our new organizations would die in infancy for want of financial support and our Foreign and Domestic missionary work would soon come to a standstill.

His remarks in this report of 1911 give us a good picture of the congregation. It was progressive and aggressive in the work of the kingdom. The church

TheRev. Martin Flipse, minister, 1913-1920.

The Rev. James M. Martin, minister, 1921-1934.

had become one of the largest Reformed churches in the Middle West, but Blekkink did not apologize for its size. Rather he saw the church as serving a useful role in advancing the cause of the Kingdom through its enthusiastic participation in missionary endeavors at home and abroad. Throughout his ministry, Third Church gained distinction in the denomination. By capitalizing on its strengths and channeling its potential in the field of Christian missions, Blekkink prevented the church from becoming a prideful institution happy in its own successes. Blekkink's zealous concern for the spiritual life of Third Church is reflected in his remark after the church was redecorated in 1912, "Paint is no substitute for piety." It was his deepest desire that the congregation of Third Church should "Know Jesus Christ as Lord and Make Jesus Christ Known to the World."[10]

V
It Was a Splendid Time

The virtual completion of the Americanization process of the Third Reformed Church came in the decade following World War I. It came through the pastoral leadership of the Rev. James M. Martin, the successor of Martin Flipse, who had served Third Church from 1913 to 1920. The choice of Martin was an unusual one in the sense that Third had chosen for its minister a person who had no link with the Dutch-American community of the Middle West. All ministers before this time had been immigrants or the children of immigrants. Mr. Martin knew no Dutch, a fact which prompted the church to leave the Holland Classis and unite with the Michigan Classis in 1921.[1] The choice of Martin was not unusual, however, in that he had been educated at Rutgers College and New Brunswick Seminary and had served pastorates in the East. Third Church had usually chosen ministers with that type of education and pastoral background. Vander Meulen, Utterwick, and Broek had been educated at Rutgers College and the theological seminary in New Brunswick; many sons of the immigrants went east in the early days for their education. Dosker had gone to the Presbyterian seminary in Chicago. Utterwick, Blekkink, and Flipse, Martin's predecessors, had had pastorates in the East. In fact, Gerrit H. Dubbink was the only minister of Third Church between 1867 and 1920 who had received the usual educational pattern for the ministers of the midwestern Dutch Reformed churches. After Hope College and Western

Theological Seminary were functioning, most midwestern ministers received their training in these institutions.

Numerical Growth

Pastor Martin was thoroughly attuned to successful American Protestantism. With his aggressive, dynamic spirit of innovation, he brought Third Church into its "golden age." It pleased the congregation greatly that the new minister sought out prospective members immediately upon assumption of his pastorate. His very persuasive manner was instrumental in garnering 144 new members by the close of his first year of ministry at Third Church. In 1922, on Martin's first Easter Sunday in Third Church, ninety-five people were received into the membership of the church. Many of these new members had come from non-Reformed churches. Pleased with the effectiveness of their pastor's methods, the congregation was in no mood to restrain Martin when he introduced innovations. He instituted the "junior sermon" in September, 1921. The Martins opened the parsonage on Sunday mornings for a church nursery. The Boy Scouts organized their first troop in Third Church in 1921.[2] The consistory approved of Pastor Martin's plan of the Every Member Canvass, a method which had been very effective in the East. However, at the congregational meeting on December 23, 1923, the congregation asked that this new procedure be postponed indefinitely. Pastor Martin even experimented with the chancel furniture and had the pulpit placed on the west side of the "platform," an "innovation which meets with general approval," according to the editor of the bulletin.[3]

Pastor Martin, who was alert to the trends of Protestant thinking in America, conveyed his interpretation of current theological movements to his congregation. On October 1, 1922, he launched a series of sermons which dealt with the major topics of the modernist-fundamentalist debate which was dominating the American religious scene. Certain elements of liberal theology in the early decades of the twentieth century had cast aspersions on some of the major doctrines of Christianity. The publication of the *Fundamentals: A Testimony to the Truth*,[4] from which the term "fundamentalism" was derived, sharpened the conflict between the proponents of liberal and conservative theology. Martin's titles for this series of sermons dealt with several of the specific topics regarded as fundamentals of the faith. The topics were:

October 1	Can Modern Civilization Accept the Miracles of the Bible?
October 8	Is it Necessary to Believe in the Virgin Birth of Jesus?
October 15	Is the Bible Still the Inspired Book, or Has Modern Scholarship Made it Untrustworthy?
October 22	Did Christ Die for the Sin of the World? If Not, What Did He Die for?
October 29	Does that First Century Promise, that Christ Will Come Again, Hold Good for the Twentieth Century?

The church bulletin editor introduced the topics by saying these questions were "agitating the church under the present attack of modernism. They are compelling us to ask whether we still can hold to the old faith of our fathers." The editor was reassuring, for he continued, "these sermons will be an attempt to show that we can."[5] Third Church did not have to worry that the minister they had imported from the East had succumbed to theological modernism. In 1925, at the time of the Scopes' trial in Tennessee which ruled against the teaching of evolution in public schools, Martin's sermon on July 26 was a discussion of evolution "from the Bible viewpoint."

Denominational Involvement

During Martin's ministry, Third Church attained unusual prominence in denominational affairs. Previous ministers had been active in the Reformed Church in America on a national level, but particular attention was focused upon this during Martin's ministry. As permanent clerk of the General Synod, Martin was required to attend the annual June meetings of the synod, occasions which afforded him the opportunity to observe the life and work of the Reformed Church in America closely. From time to time, therefore, information about the denomination would appear in the weekly church bulletin. Although many members of Third Church received denominational publications in their homes, Martin brought the affairs of the denomination to the attention of the congregation and consistently cultivated the members' interest in the life of the total denominational program. Martin's strong interest in denominational affairs was also aided by the fact that several members in the congregation had served as president of the General Synod. Since many seminary professors, retired ministers, and missionaries were members of the congregation, the bulletin writer could not fail to mention in 1926 that seven former presidents of the General Synod were members, or had been members, of Third Church.[6] They were the Rev. Dr. James F. Zwemer, retired professor of the seminary, who had died in 1921; the Rev. Dr. Evert J. Blekkink, who was then teaching at the seminary; the Rev. Dr. Peter Moerdyk, a retired minister; the Rev. Dr. Albert Oltmans, who had died in 1923, and the Rev. Dr. Samuel M. Zwemer, missionaries; and the Rev. Dr. John E. Kuizenga and and the Rev. Dr. Siebe Nettinga,[7] professors at the seminary.

With such close ties to denominational affairs, the congregation in 1921 participated wholeheartedly in the first major capital funds drive of the Reformed church. It was called the "Progress Campaign." The church's yearly quota for three years was $9,600. Third Church was one of the one hundred fourteen churches of the denomination which exceeded their quota in 1922. Immediately after this drive the Pension Fund of the denomination began its campaign for a "One Million Dollar Endowment," and the congregation again met its obligation.

The editor of the bulletin, Jacob Geerlings, was happy to note in 1923 that in total membership, Third Church was the third largest congregation in the regional Synod of Chicago of which the Holland and Michigan classes were members; it was first in Bible School enrollment; it was second in the number of families. In the words of Geerlings, this was indeed "a splendid time." He could not contain his pride concerning the prominence that Third Church had attained in the denomination as well as in the city. Geerlings impressed upon the congregation that it was one of the most successful churches of the Reformed Church in America. Third Church was a thriving, successful American Protestant congregation, conservative in theology, but abreast of the times.

Education

Other areas of the congregation's life which contributed to the glories of Third Church in this period deserve further comment. The Sunday school

The Men's Bible Class, 1912. Standing, l.-r.: Fred Helmers, John Stephan, Frank Van Ark, Wm. Vander Hart, M. Knoll, H. Vaupell, G.Du Mez, M. Vander Poel, Neal Wabeke, W. Lawrence, Nelson Pyle, Albert Brinkman, Fred Steketee, and Dr. Evert E. Blekkink; seated, l.-r: A. Borgman, M. Van Dyke, M. Van Slooten, Chris Lokker, George Dalman, John Woltman, D. J. Te Roller, Bloemendahl, J. Rutgers, Henry Geerlings, teacher, B. Dekker, H. Elferdink, H. Lievense, A. H. Meyer, De Vries, John Du Mez, Arie Woltman, H. Van Ark, C. Becker, and H. Steketee.

reached its peak with an enrollment of 1,100,[8] which included the mission Sunday school enrollment of Gibson, a small settlement south of Holland. Members of Third Church carried on work in Gibson for several years. Part of the success of the Sunday school was simply normal in that the church was in the right place at the right time and it was part of a large congregation with many children. In addition, the Sunday school had an "esprit de corps," due in part to the leadership it attracted As mentioned earlier, the prominent businessman Isaac Cappon gave twenty-two years to the Sunday school as superintendent. He was followed by Holland attorney Arend Visscher who was an active business leader in the city.[9] It was considered a privilege to serve as a teacher in the Sunday school. Moreover, Third was unlike some other churches of Dutch-immigrant descent which placed their emphasis on the catechetical program rather than on the Sunday school. In comparison with the Sunday school enrollment, the catechetical enrollment at Third was always much smaller. As a means of Christian education the Sunday school received the prime attention of the church.

Another distinctive feature of the Sunday school was the emphasis upon adult education. The high enrollment in the post-World War I period was due in part to the fact that there were as many as twelve adult classes in the Sunday school. Key leaders in the church played an active part in the adult classes. Professor Wynand Wichers of Hope College taught a women's Bible class for many years. Henry Geerlings[10] taught a men's class. During the Flipse pastorate several younger women were organized into the Gleaners' class, which was taught by Hannah Hoekje, a Bible teacher in the public schools. She was the teacher of this class for twenty-five years. The ostensible purpose of the adult classes, of course, was Christian instruction. Having so many classes certainly strengthened the lay witness of the church. But a very important side effect of the adult classes was that they served as fellowship groups within a large congregation. Adult classes had their own

The Women's Bible Class, taught by Professor Wynand Wichers, c. 1925.

officers, had social get-togethers during the week, and also had class projects. These mutual interests and projects enabled people to know one another better and played a vital part in the life of the church.

The church school also organized the congregation effectively for other purposes beyond itself. The gala annual picnics brought the entire congregation together every summer. As many as a thousand men, women, and children took the trolley to Jenison Park (now a residential area just east of the Macatawa Bay Yacht Club) for an all-day picnic. The work of the Sunday school was linked to broader ecumenical concerns through people such as Henry Geerlings, who served as president of the Michigan State Sunday School Association. During Flipse's pastorate, the Sunday school was instrumental in starting the first Daily Vacation Bible School, which had been, according to the editor of the bulletin, "...so well received in the cities." Helene Dubbink, Hannah Hoekje, Harriet Steketee, Nella Meyer, and Adelaide Borgman were pleasantly surprised that 150 children "responded" to the first summer Bible school.[11] Not least of the functions of the Sunday school in Third Church was the part it played in missionary education and the financial support of missions. As chair of missionary education, Henrietta Warnshuis rendered invaluable service.

As in many Protestant churches, the Women's Missionary Society and the Ladies' Aid involved nearly all the women of the church in some phase or phases of their activities. The missionary society provided a great quantity of equipment and supplies for missions. After working for six months in 1922-23, the missionary society shipped a large amount of material to the Amoy Mission in China for the medical work of Dr. Clarence Holleman and to the Rev. Henry and Kate Everhard De Pree. The six months' work of the society provided the following articles, as reported in the church bulletin:

> 2,855 compresses, 496 roll bandages, 69 operating garments and sheets, 156 towels, 17 pillow slips, 56 baby dresses, 53 baby blankets, 45 dolls, 5 hot water bottles, 6 dozen tooth brushes, 12 pairs of warm slippers, handkerchiefs, ribbons, and numerous arts for the school children.[12]

The bulletin editor was also pleased to announce that "the ladies have enjoyed their work."

Another organization of the women, the Ladies' Aid, had begun in 1894, two years before the missionary society. This group provided general camaradarie among the women of the church and offered opportunities for service within the congregation. This group was effectively organized with several committees, which at one time numbered as many as sixteen. The committee structure also provides an insight into the activities of the women in the Aid. There were the banquet, baked goods, apron, gown, quilt, relief, and tea committees. Still another was called "Miscellaneous" to catch anything not already covered. The Ladies' Aid often raised funds for specific purposes; in 1928 the Aid contributed $2,500 for a new organ. During the World War I period the Aid sewed materials for the Red Cross.

Music

Music was given a prominent place in the life of Third Church largely because of the efforts of John Vander Sluis, a local merchant whose work as choir director spanned the pastorates of Dosker, Dubbink, Blekkink, Flipse, and Martin.[13] The original interest in music that had begun with the Van Lente choir continued through the decades. Local newspapers, such as the *Ottawa County Times*, gave the work of the choir good coverage. Since

Ladies Aid picnic in Jenison Park, c. 1908. Mrs. Isaac Cappon is standing at the far right.

The Ladies Aid Society, c. 1915, standing in front of the east entrance of the parish hall.

the editor M. G. Manting was partial to the congregation (he attended the church), he gave much space to its activities. When the choir presented a cantata he did not just make an announcement of the coming event. He said:

> Do not miss the rendition of the beautiful cantata, "The Prophet of Nazareth," to be given at the Third Reformed Church this evening by a chorus of thirty-two voices under the direction of Chorister, John Vander Sluis.[14]

He went on to say:

> There will be solos, duets, male trio and quartet, ladies' quartet, violin selections....It will be a great treat.

During Martin's ministry, new dimensions were added to the music program of the church. The church orchestra was founded in 1927. In 1928 a new Austin organ was purchased at a cost of $16,000 to replace the first organ of the church, acquired in 1889.[15] When the old organ was

The Choir cantata, c.1910.

decommissioned, Hannah Te Roller played the doxology, since she had been one of the organists when the first organ was dedicated. She had been succeeded by Henrietta Warnshuis, who retired in 1918. Jennie Karsten was the organist at the time the new instrument was placed in the church.

Hope College

Another interesting aspect of the life of the church during James Martin's ministry was that for the first time, Hope College faculty members began to play active roles in Third Church. The faculty had traditionally been associated with the Hope Reformed Church because that church had been organized primarily for the college community and had been English speaking from the first. In spite of the fact that Third Church Americanized at a fairly rapid pace, it had not attracted many of the college families. In fact, it had lost some families to Hope Church. John H. Kleinheksel, Gerrit J. Kollen,[16] and Henry Boers, who had been members of Third Church and had been instrumental in developing its mission interests, had left the congregation for Hope Church. Henry Boers, professor of history, had taught in the Sunday school. He left Third Church in 1892 to become a member of Hope Church. Possibly for these persons, Third Church had not Americanized swiftly enough, and possibly they had preferred a congregation where the language change or the Masonic issue had been no problem. One of the first persons to break the trend of faculty association with Hope Church was Wynand Wichers. In 1909 he began his teaching career in the Hope Preparatory School and then continued at the college as a history professor, except for a period of time in the nineteen twenties when he was an officer in a local bank. He became a member of Third Church, served as a Sunday school teacher and as superintendent, and later as a consistory member. During his presidency of Hope College (1931-1945), he was the leading elder of the church. Thomas Welmers, the registrar at the college, was a member of Third Church. During Martin's pastorate two other faculty members and their families, Albert E. Lampen and Garrett E. Vander Borgh, joined the church and assumed major leadership roles in church school work and in the consistory. Clarence Kleis and his family came into the membership from First Church at the close of Martin's ministry. The association of the congregation with the college faculty members was particularly happy in that they contributed to the life of the church without dominating it. They gave the church a strong tie to the college, a school that had always been of special interest to the congregation and from which many of its young people were graduated. In 1921, when the Classis of Holland undertook support of the chair of Bible at Hope College, Third Church was one of the major contributors to this department and continued to be, even during the Depression.

Benevolences

The customary generosity of the Third Reformed Church, which had been demonstrated in various ways throughout the first fifty years of its existence, reached a high point in Martin's ministry. His enthusiasm for the projects of the denomination aroused a like enthusiasm in the congregation. The result was a new outpouring of congregational resources and gifts for denominational concerns, as well as a great variety of other benevolent causes. The outpouring of funds for others included the needy in Third's own congregation. Although Third Church had people of means in the congregation, it did not develop into a wealthy person's church. The difference in economic means among the members was indicated by the fact that many members often received help. Even prior to the Depression, many coal bills of families in need had been paid by the church. The congregation often assisted families who incurred major medical expenses. The annual report of 1924 shows that out of a total benevolent giving of $11,643.88 that year, $1,309.90 was given for local charity.

Objects of benevolent concern to which the congregation of Third Church contributed were local, national, and international in scope. In 1927 Third was one of five churches in a denomination of 741 churches to contribute over $10,000 to the boards of the Reformed Church. In the same year, the Rev. Dr. John E. Kuizenga, president of Western Theological Seminary and a member of the congregation, was happy to report that the church pledged funds for furnishing seven rooms in the new addition to the seminary dormitory.[17] At the same time, Hope College was canvassing the congregation for funds for the chapel to be built on the campus.[18] In 1927 the congregation contributed $1,000 to the Bible chair, which was occupied at the time by the Rev. Harry J. Hager, a member of the congregation.

Third Church customarily assisted new Reformed churches in getting started and building their first structures. In 1922 the congregation of the Sixth Reformed Church received $785.50 from Third Church toward the building of a new church (this congregation had been organized in the eastern part of the town in 1916). In 1928 the new congregation that formed on Van Raalte Avenue and became the Bethel Reformed Church received many members by transfer of letter, and the members who left Third received permission from the consistory to canvass Third Church members for funds with which to build a new church. When Pine Lodge was developed on the north side of Black Lake in 1925 as a youth conference site, Third Church made a contribution.

The loyalty that the church had for denominational causes did not prevent the church from contributing to almost any cause that came along. In fact, it would appear that the generosity of Third Church was well known and that anyone looking for money stopped there. The annual report of 1927 reveals that Third Church contributed also to the relief of evangelical churches in Europe, the Anti-Saloon League of Michigan, the Lord's Day Alliance, and Near East Relief. However, lest the congregation should begin to consider itself superior in its generosity, the writer of the bulletin reminded the church in 1925 that fourteen churches (out of twenty-six) in the Holland Classis exceeded Third Church in giving per family. Third Church did very well; it was generous, but it could afford to be generous considering its large membership.

The Depression

In view of the strength of Third Reformed Church under the leadership of James Martin after World War I, the writer of the bulletin, Jacob Geerlings, may be forgiven for calling it a "splendid" time. The music, the concerts, the Sunday school picnics, the increase in membership, the generosity of the congregation, the progressive innovations—all can best be described by that term used repeatedly in the Sunday bulletin, "splendid." But the splendid time came to an end rather abruptly. The Great Depression which touched every segment of American life inevitably touched Third Church. The splendid days of the nineteen twenties gave way to the depression-ridden thirties, with all of the tragedy and suffering that came to hard-pressed America.

Although church bulletins are slow to reflect the national scene, the Depression and its effects were already noted a few months after the stock market crashed in October, 1929. The announcement in the January 19, 1930, bulletin reflected the action of a congregational meeting of January 13. At the meeting of the consistory, January 6, it had been "moved and carried that the matter of organizing a Men's Relief Association be brought up at a congregational meeting and that Prof. Vander Borgh present this matter." When he presented the matter at the meeting, Vander Borgh explained how such an organization was already underway in two other denominations in the city of Holland. The congregation gave its permission to devise ways and means of organizing such a group in Third Church for aid to jobless members. In spite of the good intention of the church and its committee, there were few replies to the 300 cards of inquiry asking for the support of the organization. No further formal action was taken by the church to alleviate the economic effects of the Depression. However, as more and more members lost their jobs, the church gave funds to many families that were in need. Heads of such families were asked to do some caretaker work at the church in return. In 1932, 2,000 pounds of flour from the Red Cross were distributed among the "poor" of Third Church.

Another aspect of the life of Third Church was touched by the Depression. That, of course, was the area of finances. The ruthless economic facts of the day invariably affected the expenditures of the congregation. The minister's salary was one of the first items to be reduced. Pastor Martin accepted a $1,000 cut in his salary at the end of 1931 and another $500 in 1933, reducing his salary of $4,000 to $2,500. In September of 1932, the consistory made a point of acquainting the congregation with the "financial facts." Another victim of the reduction in expenditures was the chatty Sunday bulletin, which ceased publication from November, 1932, until 1937, and with that went a very full weekly report of the life of the congregation. In spite of the sad state of financial affairs, the consistory refused to permit any "fund-raising social activities." Stewardship was to be direct and not through fund-raising schemes.

The struggle of the consistory to meet all commitments can best be appreciated in the light of the annual report of December 31, 1933. That report had the sad news to relate that cash on hand amounted to $9.22! The current funds of the church amounted to $591.02, most of which amount was in a bank that was closed. When the Holland City Bank would open again, $258.58 in the church's account would be available. In the same bank was also a small trust fund of $323.22. The reduction of the incomes of the members was reflected in the amount which they contributed in 1933—$16,198.73—in comparison with the sum of $31,759.68 in 1926. The 1933 contributions showed a drop of almost fifty percent. The financial picture is not complete without knowledge of the fact that the church went into the Depression with a debt of $11,250 on the new organ. With cash on hand of $9.22 at the close of 1933, the size of this debt was colossal.

One unfortunate reaction in the early days of the Depression was the rebuff of Pastor Martin by the consistory. The splendid days of the nineteen twenties were over and the success of that decade could not be matched. At the meeting of the consistory on April 20, 1931, when Martin was not present, the consistory moved that the minister pay for pulpit supply when he was gone on General Synod business in his position of permanent clerk. To save money for the church in another connection, Martin was also asked to return the fees he received for "classical appointments"[19] after expenses were deducted. He was to accept no fees for funerals. There were to be no expenditures for clerical work and church expenses on his part without the approval of a committee of the consistory. Martin was also reminded to preach the points of the Heidelberg Catechism, a general custom in the Reformed church. Since the successful days were over, the minister must follow Reformed Church in America practice more carefully! A committee would also approve of the catechetical books used in his instruction classes and he was to read the "long" form[20] at communion. Some of these points invariably came up because of the state of finances, but they also show a frustration on the part of a consistory well accustomed to a successful church in meeting the needs of the moment. An attack on the minister gave them an outlet for their frustrations and troubles. Martin resigned his pastorate at Third Church in the spring of 1934. It was the longest pastorate in the history of Third Church and, except for the Depression troubles, one of great significance.

Third Church discovered that the departure of Pastor Martin did not bring the solution to its problems that the consistory might have anticipated in its action of April, 1931. The church was "vacant"[21] for more than two years. Pastoral supply, of course, was no problem, since among the members of Third Church were many ministers who could conduct Sunday services. The congregation called a Presbyterian minister, James Veneklasen, who declined. The church then attempted to get some of the bright young ministers in the Middle West to serve the congregation. John R. Mulder, professor of preaching at the seminary and one of the most gifted preachers of his generation, declined a call also. Two other young pastors in the early

The Christian Endeavor pageant, "Follow the Gleam,"1935. Three members of the pageant are members of Third Church in 1995: Barbara Lampen, standing far left; Thelma Kooiker Leenhouts, seated at the feet of the "king"; and Marie Dalman Van Eerden, seated at far right.

The Rev. William Van't Hof, minister, 1936-1945.

years of their ministries also declined the invitation to serve Third Church, William Goulooze, minister of the Eighth Reformed Church in Grand Rapids, and Richard C. Oudersluys,[22] minister of the First Reformed Church in Milwaukee. In the meantime, a seminary graduate, Victor Maxam, served the church on an interim basis. Finally, the church turned once more to the Reformed church in the East for a new minister, the Rev. William Van't Hof, who assumed the pastorate in November, 1936.

The Church Building

The symbol of the decline of the successful congregation during the Depression can be seen in what happened to the church building. In fact,

The parsonage, 1872-1913.

The parsonage, 1913-1960.

The exterior of Third Church as it appeared from 1921 to 1952.

the building had already suffered in the prosperous period of the 1920s. If it had not been for the Depression, the church building would have been demolished and a new one erected in its place. When the interior of the church was redecorated in 1921, the exterior also underwent considerable change, and from an aesthetic point of view, an unfortunate change. Red brick siding was placed around the lower part of the church to a height of approximately four or five feet, destroying the simple beauty of the exterior lines of the church. The two front entrances were removed and replaced with brick entrances that did not match the general lines of the church. Instead of repairing the vertical batten boards, a "Kellystone" surface was placed over them, changing completely the outer appearance of the church. The interior did not suffer in the redecorating process; it continued to possess the lovely bright motifs that characterized the 1912 redecoration. There was a strong sentiment at the time in favor of removing the original pews, but by a vote of 86 for and 161 against, the original pews were retained. Possibly the exterior changes of the church were regarded as temporary, for in a few years a movement was under way to build a new church. "The New Building Fund" was inaugurated in 1925. The editor of the bulletin attempted to encourage contributions to the building fund by saying:

> And the faster [the nest egg] grows the sooner will Third Church people enjoy the comforts and advantages of a building commensurate with the place it occupies as one of the largest churches in the Reformed Church in America.[23]

The fund did not grow rapidly; possibly the cost of a new organ superseded the need for a building fund. At any rate, the Depression stifled all thoughts of building a new church. Instead, during the period when Third did not have an installed pastor, 1934-1936, a major remodeling program took place

The interior of Third Church as it appeared from 1935 to 1952.

which altered the interior of the church as much as the 1921 program had altered the exterior. In line with the decorating trends of the nineteen thirties, the interior of the church was painted in dark colors and the brightly painted plaster ceiling was converted to one of dark green acoustical tiles. After this redecorating was completed, the appearance of the church, from either an interior or exterior point of view, had little semblance to the original church. All of the "improvements" in these two decades virtually destroyed the beauty of the building, both inside and out.

Recovery

The task of carrying the congregation through the trying days of the Depression was given to the new minister, the Rev. William Van't Hof. He was able to recover the momentum the church had acquired in the decade after World War I under Martin's ministry and carry it through his pastorate, from 1936 to 1945, in spite of the economic troubles of the country. By the close of 1939 the mortgage had been wiped out and funds were collected for an ambitious building program. At a congregational meeting in May of 1941, it was moved to construct a two-story educational building and to install a new heating system for the entire church, at the estimated cost of $40,000. But Depression caution led to the church's decision not to begin the new project until $30,000 of the cost was in hand. In case of economic reversals, the church did not intend to be caught with a large mortgage again. When war broke out in 1941, though money was being raised for building purposes, all plans for a new building program were cancelled.

In an effort to unite and strengthen the church after its long period of difficulties and its years without a pastor, Pastor Van't Hof devoted his full attention to his pastoral duties. In 1938 he made 543 calls among the members of the congregation. He had to examine the membership rolls and bring them up to date. Many of the members who had joined the church during Martin's pastorate had either moved away or had become inactive; hence the revised membership roll of the church showed a decline. But the new minister's intense pastoral concerns and his prodigious pastoral activity brought many new members into the church, so that by the conclusion of Van't Hof's ministry, 524 new members had joined Third Church, an average of more than fifty a year. During Van't Hof's ministry he made in

The seventy-fifth anniversary dinner held in Carnegie Gymnasium on the Hope College campus, October 13, 1942.

excess of 5,000 calls. Pastor Van't Hof's salary stayed at the same $3,000 level with which he began his ministry at Third Church, although it is true that the consistory allowed him the help of guest ministers regularly. His reward for hard work had to be the loving response of the people rather than dollars. Some part-time help was given him, but Pastor Van't Hof sustained the large burden of pastoral work himself.

The love of the congregation for Mr. Van't Hof was indicated by the respect it had for him in spite of his pacifist position. There was no mention of the United States' entry into the war in the December 14, 1941, bulletin and, until a number of young people were serving in the armed forces, church bulletins seldom made reference to the war. But it was made known to the congregation, without causing any dissent, that any young people of the church who "wish to be considered conscientious objectors to combatant miltary service" could register their names with the vice-president of the consistory.[24] One hundred eighty-eight members of Third Church served in the armed forces during World War II.

Easter Sunday, 1945.

Ladies Aid dinner, March 19, 1940.

With the conclusion of the pastorate of the Rev. William Van't Hof on Easter Sunday, April 1, 1945, another major period in the life of the congregation had come to a close. Americanization was no longer a major question, that is, an Americanization which generally blended the Dutch-immigrant Protestant into the cultural and religious scene of the United States. Third Church had become a typical American Protestant congregation, a successful city church, similar to many conservative Protestant churches in countless cities throughout America. Among the churches of immigrant background in Holland, Michigan, Third Church was foremost in this kind of Americanization.

VI
Renewal and Restoration

"An old people's church" was the description applied to the Third Reformed Church in the period following World War II. The congregation had been affected by the population changes in the city of Holland following the war. Returning servicemen brought a building boom causing a suburban sprawl, a situation experienced by many cities and towns in the United States. As the boundaries of the city continued to spread, the younger families of the church began to live farther away and to join churches near their homes. To meet the suburban need for churches in the decade of the forties, the Maplewood Reformed Church was organized by the Classis of Holland on the south side of the town in 1941, and in 1944 the Beechwood Reformed Church was organized on the north side; in 1951 the Calvary Reformed Church was organized on the east side of the city.[1] Third Church, in pattern set by the classis, aided these churches not only with funds but also in the transfer of some members. All of these congregations flourished almost immediately, but at the expense of the downtown churches such as Third Church.

When the new minister, the Rev. Dr. Jacob J. Sessler, arrived in 1946, having come from the College Point Reformed Church, Long Island, New York, he came to a church with a declining membership and a falling Sunday school enrollment. During his ministry there was a net loss of 100 members. Third Church was facing a problem which many city churches had faced earlier: a population mobility which was bound to affect the size of the congregation and Sunday school despite the presence of a very gifted minister in the pulpit. It has always been the tendency in such changes to make the minister the scapegoat, to account for such losses, but Third Church did not do that to Dr. Sessler. The new minister was nationally recognized as an excellent preacher and author. The congregation deeply regretted his early resignation in 1949 on account of ill health.

The postwar period was a time of general frustration for the congregation. A new building program or the refurbishing of the sanctuary was needed, as well as a new educational unit and parish hall. Plans were made but nothing was done. A petition signed by 121 persons was presented to the consistory requesting that "in view of the present unsightly appearance of the exterior of the auditorium section of the church some immediate steps should be taken to rectify this condition. . . ." New stained glass windows were placed

The Rev. Dr. Jacob J. Sessler, minister, 1946-1949.

in the sanctuary in 1946,[2] with the idea that they could be removed when a new church would be built.

The church did recognize the need for pastoral assistance on a regular basis, but there were difficulties here. Elizabeth Renskers Koeppe[3] served as a general pastoral assistant for two years, but she returned to the mission field in China with her husband, Edwin, in 1946. Geraldine Smies, the first full-time director of Christian education, replaced her but had to resign in 1947 because of ill health. Harold De Roo worked at the church while attending Western Seminary, 1947-48. The church liked his work very much and called him to serve on a full-time basis after his graduation. He was ordained and installed in September of 1948, but, much to the disappointment of the congregation, he resigned in June of 1949 to take a pastorate in Redlands, California.

The Rev. Harold P. De Roo, associate minister, 1948-1949.

Ecumenicity

In early 1947 the church had a minor struggle on the issue of ecumenicity. The Rev. Henry Bast had written a pamphlet entitled "An Appeal to the Ministers and Laymen of the Chicago and Iowa Synods [of the Reformed Church in America]." He called into question the Reformed church's membership in the Federal Council of Churches, which had always been a suspect organization in the eyes of many ministers and churches in the western part of the denomination. The attack by Bast on the Federal Council was not the first one made on it; overtures to the General Synod appeared from time to time calling for the Reformed church to withdraw from this body which represented the majority of Protestantism in the United States. Under the leadership of Dr. Sessler, the consistory of Third Church voted to continue its membership in the Federal Council and backed its determination with a contribution. The token sum of five dollars was voted to the Federal Council, the size of the gift possibly indicating a lack of enthusiasm for the Federal Council by the entire consistory, but at least the consistory was willing to stand up and be counted on this issue. The faculties of both New Brunswick and Western Seminaries made pronouncements simultaneously in favor of the Reformed church affiliation with the Federal Council. While this matter was under discussion in Third Church, Dr. Sessler also encouraged a positive view on the proposed merger proceedings of the Reformed church with the United Presbyterian church. On November 23, 1947, the Rev. Arthur R. Armstrong of the United Presbyterian Church of New Kensington, Pennsylvania, was a guest minister at Third Church. By vote of the consistory, Pastor Sessler and Elder Peter Notier were instructed to express at a special meeting of the classis a favorable inclination toward merger. At a later congregational meeting on the subject of merger, eighty members voted for merger and ninety-six against it. The western part of the Reformed church voted down the merger by a larger percentage. There was, however, some recognition in Third Church that the age of ecumenicity had come.

In spite of the disappointment over the brevity of Dr. Sessler's pastorate, Third Church was fortunate in obtaining new pastoral leadership quickly. In fact, with the coming of his successor, the Rev. Christian H. Walvoord from Hudson, New York, in 1950, Third Church entered an era of renewal. The spirit of renewal also characterized the pastorate of his successor, the Rev.

Russell Vande Bunte, so that the final period of the church's first century (1950-1967) was a bright one. Beginning with Mr. Walvoord's pastorate, there developed a new outlook in church affairs, a reawakening of the progressive spirit that had marked some earlier periods, an enlargement of the church's vision, and a complete rebuilding and restoration of the church's entire physical plant.

Worship

On the denominational level, a liturgical renewal was taking place under the impetus of the leadership of the Rev. Dr. Howard G. Hageman of Newark, New Jersey. The general indifference of the Reformed Church in America to liturgy is evidenced by the fact that no attempt at revision of the liturgy of the denomination had been made since 1906. A survey of the order of the morning and evening worship services printed in the church bulletin of Third Church from 1915 to 1950 indicates an indifferent approach to liturgy, typical of most midwestern Reformed churches. Since the Rev. Dr. Richard C. Oudersluys, a member of the congregation, was a member of the commission on liturgy of the denomination, it was appropriate that, when the first revision appeared in 1952, Third Church show its appreciation of the denomination's attempt to improve the pattern of worship in the Reformed churches. Accordingly, Pastor Walvoord, with the recommendation of the worship committee, led the consistory to adopt the newly revised liturgy of the Reformed church. Ten years later, in 1962, Third Church adopted the completed liturgical forms which the denomination's committee had produced and which the General Synod had voted to adopt. At this time, Pastor Vande Bunte was a member of the commission on liturgy. Third Church, however, had been among the minority of churches in the western Reformed church to use the new liturgical forms approved by the denomination.

Third's spirit of willingness to adopt the new was true in other areas: in the use of the Revised Standard Version (RSV) of the Bible and in the use of the new *Hymnbook*. By 1956 Third Church was using in the Sunday school the Revised Standard Version of the Bible which had been published in 1952. The RSV had been severely maligned by many Protestant ministers and laypersons including Reformed church pastors. Many critics of the new version felt that the Word of God had been abandoned to the "higher critics"

The Rev. Christian H. Walvoord, senior minister, 1950-1958.

and "modernists" and therefore the new revision was untrustworthy. Third not only adopted the RSV in the Sunday school but at a later time, without controversy, for use in the pulpit and the pew as well.

The new *Hymnbook* was readily accepted at Third Church. It had been produced by five cooperating denominations, including the Reformed church, in 1955. While the majority of the Reformed churches in the western synods used a hymnal called the *Service Hymnal*, which consisted largely of revivalistic hymns and gospel songs, Third Church went beyond this "fundamentalizing" influence. Under the leadership of Walvoord and Vande Bunte, the worship of the church was revitalized with the adoption of the new liturgy, the Revised Standard Version of the Bible, and the new

Hymnbook, a position which sets it quite apart from most midwestern Reformed churches, many of which have adopted none of these. The question here was no longer whether the church be Dutch or American; the question was whether the church would reflect the midwestern affinity for American Protestant Fundamentalism or use the recommended forms and hymns of the Reformed church and its tradition.

Christian Education

Beginning with the new period under Walvoord and Vande Bunte, the program of Christian education underwent considerable change. Groundwork for such change had been laid during Pastor Van't Hof's service at Third Church by formation of a Christian Education Council in 1938. The purpose of the council was to coordinate the total program of Christian education which formerly had been carried primarily by the Sunday school. Initially the council had the trouble of finding its niche in the structure of the organizational life of the church, but after growing pains, it became an influential committee in the church. Shortly after Walvoord began his ministry at Third, the junior church was inaugurated to allow the children from the kindergarten through the fourth grade to have their own worship service in the chapel during a part of the adult service in the sanctuary.

With the support of the Christian Education Council, Walvoord was able to convince the consistory that an addition to the fulltime staff was not a luxury, but a necessity. Roger Rietberg was engaged to direct the youth program and to serve as minister of music in 1950. He was succeeded in the youth program by Mary Blair Bennett, Phyllis Luidens, and then by an associate minister, the Rev. Jerry Veldman. The Christian Education Council, therefore, followed precedent when it urged the calling of the the Rev. Mark Walvoord in 1967 as an associate pastor with responsibilities in Christian education.

The council also adopted the new Covenant Life Curriculum in 1964 when it was first issued by the denomination in cooperation with the Southern Presbyterian church. This was a courageous move, because again the majority of the midwestern Reformed church considered the material suspect, as it was open to new trends in biblical studies which assumed that higher criticism was here to stay and possibly contributed to a better

The Rev. Jerry A. Veldman, minister, 1955-1962.

understanding of the Bible. The high quality of this material was evident and the church adopted it immediately.

Administration

A new day also came to Third Church through the administrative leadership of the Rev. Christian Walvoord. In 1952, Pastor Walvoord set up a contemporary church office, with adequate office equipment, and employed a full-time church secretary. His predecessors had traditionally had their office/studies in the parsonage next door to the church. Then he published a guide for administrative procedures. His "Manual of Church Operation" was a thorough exposition of the operation of an up-to-date church of the nineteen fifties. The administrative abilities of Mr. Walvoord poured over into other areas that brought renewal and change to the church. In 1956 he induced the church to make a self-study of the congregation to better understand the changes taking place in Holland and to make some preparations for the future. The actual outcome of the study was only the purchase of two lots and homes west of the church on Thirteenth Street for more parking space next to the church, but the committee had been confronted with the fact that the population of Holland was mobile and that new people were coming to Holland who needed to be reached with the gospel. In spite of the new and dynamic minister, church membership and Sunday school enrollment continued to recede slowly. Although the self-study commission did not come up with startling solutions, Pastor Walvoord personally made very sincere efforts to recruit new members to Third

The church staff, 1958
Seated, l.-r. Mrs. Robert Beukema, Mildred W. Schuppert, and Barbara Lampen; standing, l.-r. the Rev. Christian H. Walvoord, Roger Rietberg, Jacob Klomparens, and the Rev. Jerry A. Veldman.

Church from the personnel moving to town to work in the new General Electric plant on East Sixteenth Street. At this time, as for some years previously, Third Church was receiving "competition" for new members. Hope Church, because of its broad-minded and open attitude toward people who were not of Dutch extraction, had become the leading Protestant church in the city. During the ministry of the Rev. Dr. Marion de Velder at Hope Church, 1939 to 1959, nearly thirty members transferred from Third Church to Hope Church. Strangely enough, a group of members also filtered over to the very conservative Immanuel Baptist Church, which had become a prominent, fundamentalistic church in the community. The Holland area was changing in complexion and Walvoord sensed this. Through his determined efforts, several "General Electric people" joined Third Church. At that time the membership of Third Church had stabilized; communicant members numbered about 800.

Women's Guild

The women's work of the church received new organizational expression under the direction of Marie Verduin Walvoord, the pastor's wife. The Ladies' Aid and Missionary Society had been augmented with a group of younger women who called themselves the Women's Mission Auxiliary. In 1955 these three groups were organized into one Women's Guild which combined the activities and interests of the three former groups. Dorothy Welch Stephens was elected president of the new organization.[4] The missionary interest in the church, which had always been promoted by the women in the missionary societies, was transferred to the new society through continued financial support and occasional missionary speakers. The circle units within the large guild were named after missionaries serving actively in the mission field. Some members of the guild who wished to retain a distinct mission emphasis were accepted as one of the "interest" units, and ardent adherents of the Ladies' Aid were recognized as another interest group and called the Friendly Sewing Circle. But the transition was made smoothly and enthusiastically to the new organizational framework. The pattern established by the Women's Guild in Third Church was used as a model by the National Department of Women's Work of the Reformed Church in America when it revised its program of women's work in the denomination in 1957.

The Gleaners' Class fiftieth anniversary dinner, 1965.

Stewardship

Under Christian Walvoord's leadership, the church was able to overcome its Depression attitude in the matter of church finances. The consistory had become extremely cautious in raising funds and parsimonious in spending church monies, because of its experience at the time of the Depression. The consistory was also extremely cautious in the raising of the minister's salary. The prominence of the church in denominational affairs and the exceptional demands the church made upon its ministerial leadership was not reflected in the salaries paid to the ministers until the mid-sixties. Although the salary scale reflected a cautious mood, Walvoord was able to set the sights of the church at a much higher level in regard to stewardship. By 1957 the congregation was back in the pre-Depression swing of adequate and healthy giving. During that year, the benevolent giving of the church reached $35,000, which was distributed to seventy-five missionaries, mission causes, and a great variety of other benevolent causes. The early generous spirit of the church was renewed in this decade. In the decade of the nineteen sixties the church again resumed a significant generosity to Hope College. In 1927 it had contributed to the new chapel,[5] in 1939 to the new science building,[6] and in 1962 it made a pledge to the new physics-math building.[7] In the five-year period from 1962 to 1967, the church contributed approximately $13,500 to the capital budget of Hope College and $31,000 to the operating budget. The total giving of the congregation to all causes in 1957 almost reached the $90,000 mark and, in 1967, the $144,000 mark.

An interesting project of the church in mission outreach was the financing of the building of the Riverford Heights Reformed Church in Detroit. The idea of assisting an extension church had come from members of the church who had attended a men's convention in Chicago in November, 1956. The outcome of this project was that Third Church loaned this new congregation $50,000. Then, the members of Third Church proceeded to contribute $43,795.50 to the Riverford Heights fund, repaying the loan in effect, and at a congregational meeting on February 3, 1965, the congregation cancelled all remaining indebtedness of the new congregation to Third Church. A new Reformed church not in the Holland area had become the recipient of the church's generosity to the amount of $50,000. In turn, Third Church's mission zeal was somewhat revived by this venture.[8]

Christian Life

In this time of renewal, old conservative opinions were slowly giving way to some change. The temperance issue was not raised after the repeal of the 18th amendment, though the Women's Christian Temperance Union had been very active in the church prior to the Depression. The Sabbath question had occasionally come to the fore prior to World War II. The church, along with others in the community, had expressed its opposition to the opening of the movie theaters on Sunday. In 1941, the consistory had protested the seven-day defense program of President Franklin D. Roosevelt on sabbatarian grounds. It had also expressed dissatisfaction with the Sunday commercialism that the Tulip Time festival was bringing to Holland. But in 1965 when the Classis of Holland was attempting to keep the new Windmill Island closed on Sundays, the consistory did not agree with the position taken by the classis.

The consistory slowly moved from a position of rigorous oversight of the morals of the community and the congregation to a more moderate position. Social dancing received no more condemnation from the elders after the 1918 incident. The elders of the church regarded divorce by church members a very serious offense. In the post World War I period they would not allow a divorced person who had remarried to take communion, if the divorce were not on "biblical" grounds. This was still the position taken by

The Rev. Russell W. Vande Bunte, senior minister, 1959-1969.

the elders in 1940. Later the consistory moderated its position, leaving to the pastor's judgment the decision as to whether remarriage could be permitted. The old Masonry conflict remained an undercurrent in the church; it was understood that no man could be elected to a consistory position if he were a member of a lodge. When in 1928, the much respected and well-known community leader Henry Geerlings was elected to serve as elder, certain members asked him not to accept the position because he was a Mason. As a result of this rebuff by some people in the congregation, he graciously declined to serve,[9] and later transferred his membership to Hope Church. But the old questions which had long taxed the church, such as membership in a lodge, Christian conduct on the Sabbath, and the question of personal social life, have not agitated the church after World War II; and the congregation seems finally to have outgrown them.

More momentous questions faced the congregation when the Civil Rights movement developed. The response of the church to these more crucial questions was lukewarm, although the consistory approved the Open Housing Covenant of 1964. Pastoral leadership by Vande Bunte attempted to overcome apathy on questions of major social import—questions which

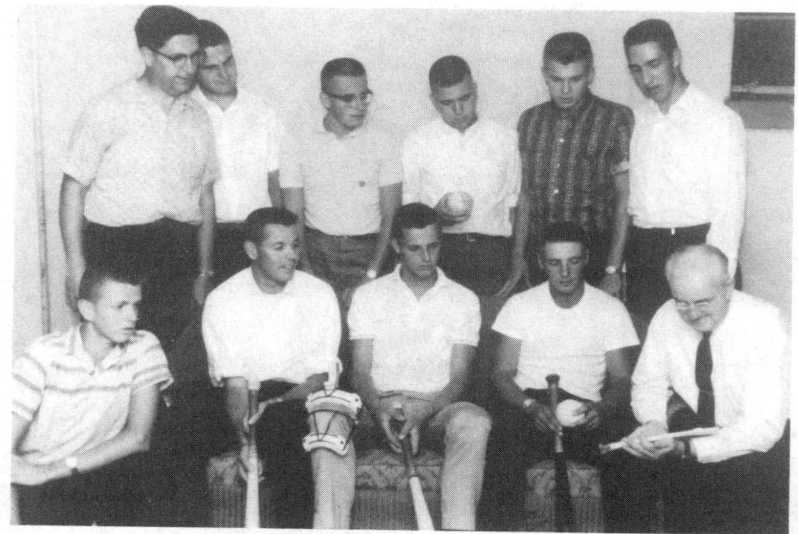

The young men's baseball team with pastors Vande Bunte and Veldman.

far outweigh those of sabbath observance and lodge membership, which had been inherited from a previous generation and are still considered important by many in Holland, Michigan.

Property Improvements

The renewal of the life of the church during the pastorate of Christian Walvoord and Russell Vande Bunte was accompanied by improvements in the physical structure of the church. Because of the illness of Jacob Sessler, the planned postwar building program had not been realized during his pastorate. When Walvoord came, the new building project moved ahead immediately. The first major project was the replacement of the old parish hall with a new Christian education building. This program was finished in 1952 at a cost of $253,000. The church building also received some necessary attention. In November, 1949, James K. Haveman submitted a plan to remove the two brick front entrances of the church and to replace them with one main entrance cut into the direct center of the north end of

The Christian Education building, 1952-1994.

the sanctuary, and then to cover the entire exterior of the building with limestone and brick to match the new parish hall. This proposed plan to further disfigure the church was fortunately rejected. Instead, the ugly Kellystone exterior of the church was removed and the original side boards with batten strips exposed. The brick siding of 1921 was not removed. Nevertheless, there was a marked improvement in the appearance of the exterior of the church.

Soon after the arrival of Pastor Walvoord, and while the building of the Christian education unit was in progress, the church was confronted with an unusual opportunity. Chancel furniture which had been in the St. Nicholas[10] Church of New York City before it was razed in 1948 was offered to Third Church. The Rev. Dr. Joseph R. Sizoo, who had assumed the pastorate in St. Nicholas in 1936, felt it necessary to replace the ornate Victorian pulpit furniture. Since many of his parishioners were of Episcopalian background, he followed an Anglican arrangement for the new chancel. Because the Collegiate consistory was unwilling to assume the expense, Dr. Sizoo was required to raise the funds himself in order to make this change. One

The exterior of Third Church, 1952-1967.

contributor was Mrs. Robert Todd Lincoln, who had been a parishioner in the New York Avenue Presbyterian Church in Washington, D.C., where Sizoo served from 1924 to 1936. The daughter-in-law of President Abraham Lincoln, who with his family had attended the New York Avenue church during his presidency, said to Dr. Sizoo when she presented her gift, "I would like to give you a sum of money to erect in your church a pulpit which

The interior of Third Church, 1952-1967.

will commemorate your relationship with the Lincoln family."[11] As a result, the beautiful chancel furniture was carved for the St. Nicholas Church by Italian craftsmen in 1936.

After World War II the Collegiate Church consistory received an offer from a corporation to buy the church and lease the property for the construction of a fifty-story skyscraper. The price offered for the church was $3,750,000! Since the church, which had been erected in 1869, still carried a large mortgage, and since it was in need of major repairs, the Collegiate consistory accepted the offer, with the intention of rebuilding in the "fashionable east-seventies." Dr. Sizoo disagreed completely with the proposed sale of the St. Nicholas Church. In protest to the sale, he resigned his pastorate in 1947 and became the president of the New Brunswick Theological Seminary. The church building was demolished in 1949 and the chancel furniture was placed in storage. After the offer of the St. Nicholas chancel furniture was made to Third Church, the congregation, at a meeting held July 12, 1951, accepted the gift. The furniture was installed in Third Church during the time the new educational building was being constructed. The furnishings which had been designed for the stone, Victorian Gothic-type structure of St. Nicholas Church found an acceptable setting in the carpenters' Gothic interior of Third. The congregation had Americanized sufficiently so that it could accept Episcopalian chancel furnishings in its Reformed church sanctuary!

The next building project of the congregation was the acquisition of a new parsonage. The parsonage which had been built following the Holland fire in 1871 had served until 1913 when it was sold and moved to 280 East 8th Street. The church then purchased a home directly west of that parsonage, owned by Prof. Henry Boers, who had died the previous year. During the nineteen fifties this dwelling had already been considered inadequate. At the time of the Vande Bunte family's arrival in 1959, plans were ready to build a new parsonage. The excavation was already completed when the home of Mr. and Mrs. Henry Maentz at 134 West Twelfth Street became available for purchase, property immediately adjacent to Third Church. The home had been built after World War I by Mr. and Mrs. Gerrit J. Diekema, a Holland attorney and his wife, who at the time of his death in 1930 was serving as the United States Minister Plenipotentiary to the Netherlands. The magnificent home was purchased at a price much less than its value and after renovation became the new parsonage of Third Church, the fourth home used to house the minister of the congregation.

Sanctuary Restoration

One major building project remained, namely, the sanctuary. Since the large building project of 1952 and the new parsonage were paid for, the church was ready to make a decision about the building of a new church. It was obvious that both the exterior and interior of the sanctuary demanded major attention. Furthermore, it was found that the mortar of the foundation had lost its bond, that the church was in fact resting on piles of stone and sand. A new foundation was imperative. The architectual firm of Kammeraad and Stroop, engaged to study the physical structure of the church and to make recommendations for effecting necessary and desirable improvements, presented its first plan to the consistory on August 3, 1964. Indicating their appreciation of the beauty of the ninety-year-old sanctuary, the architects

The parsonage, showing the north side of the Christian education building in the background.

recommended the building of a new church, patterned after the old building. However, in an appearance before the consistory on November 2, 1964, at the personal invitation of Pastor Vande Bunte, the Rev. Dr. Donald J. Bruggink, a professor of church history at the seminary, a specialist in Reformed church architecture, and a member of the congregation, urged the consideration of the restoration of the old building. In response to this suggestion, in February, 1965, the consistory appointed a committee under the direction of Henry Ten Pas to consider the entire matter.

On the basis of the historical significance of the sanctuary (the second oldest church building in Holland, Michigan), its architectural integrity, and its aesthetic quality, the committee in May, 1966, proposed to the congregation that the sanctuary be restored. The proposal met with a considerable difference of opinion (especially because a new structure of the same size could be built at approximately the same cost). However, at

A view of the back of the sanctuary prior to the restoration of 1967-1968.

a congregational meeting on June 22, 1966, the proposal to restore the church passed by a vote of 204 to 59. The church was saved, although the new plan reversed the idea of replacing the old church with a new one, an idea which had been under consideration since 1925. The reversal of this intention of forty-one years may well be considered another instance of Americanization. It is a well-known fact that immigrants go through a cycle that sees the first generation trying to preserve the language and customs of the mother country, then the second and third generations trying to shake off the "stigma" of their origin. The cycle reaches its conclusion when people feel themselves sufficiently secure to be sensitive to those things in their past which have lasting value. One evidence of the security of the members of Third Church as an American congregation can be seen in their sensitivity to the beauty of the church built by their ancestors and their determination to see it restored.

New foundations under construction, 1967.

The restoration project was underway at the time the congregation entered its centennial year with the attendant festivities marking the 100th anniversary of the church. The restoration included the removal of the red brick siding and the entrances which had been added in 1921 and the elimination of most of the aspects of the interior decoration project of 1935. The exterior of the church was fully restored to resemble as much as possible its original appearance. Quite to everyone's surprise, both the tower and the side boards and battens proved to be in a remarkable state of preservation. Because a new foundation was a necessity, the occasion was used to completely excavate the area beneath the sanctuary and to create additional new space for the Christian education program. Since the floor structure had also been adjudged by the architects to be inadequate, a new reinforced concrete floor was laid, over which wide, soft wood boards, like the original flooring, were placed.

Commensurate with the attempt to retain as much of the original structure as possible, all of the marvelous carpenters' Gothic pillars and arches were retained, as well as the original pews (albeit cushions were added as a concession to contemporary standards of comfort). While an exact description of the original decoration was unobtainable, the attempt was made to decorate in a manner commensurate with the original.

Several areas posed insuperable problems for restoration of what was to continue as a functioning church home. The decision to maintain the original exterior appearance necessitated meeting contemporary needs for narthex space, coat racks, and two stairways to the balcony in the interior. This was accomplished by using the space of two small interior entrances plus that of the "overflow-lecture room" with its vertical sliding walls to separate it from the sanctuary, for the above purposes. The two spiralled staircases, while original to the present alterations, were done in a style that would allow them to blend in with the style of the church. For lighting, the lanterns of the 1935 period were retained. From the very beginning, Ten Pas's committee had been given to understand that the rich stained glass windows of 1946 and the Lincoln-Sizoo-St. Nicholas chancel furniture would be maintained—and they were. A new rose window was placed in the north end of the sanctuary by the grandchildren of George and Lena Oosting Mooi, in their grandparents' memory. The $375,000 building renewal program was accomplished within one percent of estimated cost. The entire program was completed in April, 1968. The cornerstone was set in place May 5, and a service of rededication was conducted May 12, 1968.

A historic building of considerable beauty was thus saved and restored. It ranks as the third oldest among the architecturally significant and historic public buildings in Holland, Michigan, preceded only by the Pillar Church, built in 1856, and Van Vleck Hall on the Hope College campus, built in 1857. It is not without merit that the claim can be made that the restoration of the historic sanctuary led to the renewal and restoration of many homes in the neighborhood and in the city. Graves Hall on the college campus had been restored just previous to Third Church, however. The church was placed on the National Register of Historic Places through the successful efforts of Willard C. Wichers, a member of the congregation and the Michigan Historical Commission. Much of the neighborhood of Third Church is now a Historic District. The Cappon Home at Washington Boulevard and Ninth Street was restored in the 1980s and is now a museum, open to the public. Much of Holland's downtown has been restored. On the college campus, Van Vleck Hall, Voorhees Hall, and the president's home have been

Restoration in progress, December 29, 1967.

restored. The old city post office became the home of the Holland Museum in 1992, following a complete restoration and modernization of this classic building. Instead of destroying Holland's significantly historic buildings like the Albertus and Christina Van Raalte home on the east side or the historic

A church pew, number 76, in use since 1875.

Manting home on the south side, the civic-minded and historically sensitive citizens of Holland, Michigan, joined Third Church members in restoring rather than destroying beautiful and worthy old structures.

At the dedication of the church following the restoration, the old communion set was given a place of honor. The silver pitcher or flagon was a gift to Third Church in 1875 by L. D'Ooge, father of Mrs. Henry Utterwick, whose husband was the pastor from 1872 to 1880. The Hope Reformed Church presented the four communion cups in November, 1873. The four plates were added by the congregation. After the church changed to the individual communion cups about 1912, the consistory gave the set to the Dutch-immigrant congregation of Dog Pound, Alberta, Canada (now called the Bottrell Community Church). That church in turn gave the flagon and two cups to another congregation in Edmonton. During the intervening years, two cups and a plate were lost. Upon the request of the Historical Committee, these churches graciously consented to give up the communion set in recognition of Third's centennial celebration. The set was restored to its original beauty by Mildred W. Schuppert in memory of her parents, I. Thomas and Alwine Mielke Schuppert.

In the restored church, Third Reformed Church bears the marks of a variety of emphases in worship since its construction in 1874. Like most churches coming out of the Reformation, its primary emphasis is upon the hearing of the Word. Originally built, Third Church followed the typical nineteenth century pattern of having a central pulpit mounted on a stage, behind which was the choir loft. The pipes of the organ filled the chancel arch. Since seating for the congregation was governed by the pragmatic consideration of how the greatest numbers could be seated as near the pulpit as possible, and since the pulpit was central, the pews were massed in front of the pulpit, eliminating the center aisle. The pews, placed in 1875, have numbers on the ends which are a reminder of the days when most Protestant churches in America financed a large part of their budgets through the rental of pews. Families rented their pews for the year, and in return possessed veritable title to them. The custom was abandoned at the turn of the century because of the conviction that the church and its pews should be open to all without consideration of financial ability to contribute to the church.

With the acquisition of the liturgical furniture of the St. Nicholas Church, the disposition of worship was markedly changed. The choir was no longer tiered in full view of the congregation, and the minister no longer had a stage on which to perform. The minister did, however, receive a pulpit which by its size and the quality of its carving made it a dignified and imposing place from which to proclaim God's Word. The lectern, formerly essential to episcopal worship, is largely superfluous in Reformed worship, except as a place for an assistant in the service, or for a lay reader.

Behind the table, against the rear wall, is a presbyter's bench. In the early church the elders, or presbyters, sat at one end of the worship room. Among them was the leading elder, or bishop, who taught, while together they

Detail in the carving on the chancel pulpit which was commissioned for the St. Nicholas Collegiate Church, New York City, by Mrs. Robert Todd Lincoln in 1936.

served at the table. Thus it is fitting within Reformed church order that the presbyter's bench be used both by the ministers and by the elders. This bench was constructed from an extra choir pew of the St. Nicholas chancel furniture.

The table, which in a medieval Catholic setting was placed against the dossal cloth at the far wall, has been moved to a more suitable position for Reformed worship. It now stands as close as possible to the congregation, and the minister can lead much of the worship service from behind the table. This custom goes back to the earliest days of the church and was practiced as well by John Calvin, who saw the table as a suitable place from which to worship because of the association of the Lord's Supper with the mediating death of Christ.

The cup, flagon, and plate on the table remind us of the sacrament of the Lord's Supper. While most of the Reformation churches have never

The chancel choir, 1968.

The congregation at worship, 1968.

followed the wishes of their theological leaders in returning to the New Testament practice of a weekly celebration of the Supper, nonetheless it is hoped that these symbols may play some part in reminding the members week by week of their participation in the death and resurrection of Christ.[12]

Since the restoration was in process when the congregation celebrated the 100th anniversary of the founding of the church, centennial activities were marked with a congregational dinner in the Civic Center on Saturday, September 9, 1967, at which time a pageant depicting scenes of the old days was presented under the direction of Marie Kruithof, who, with her

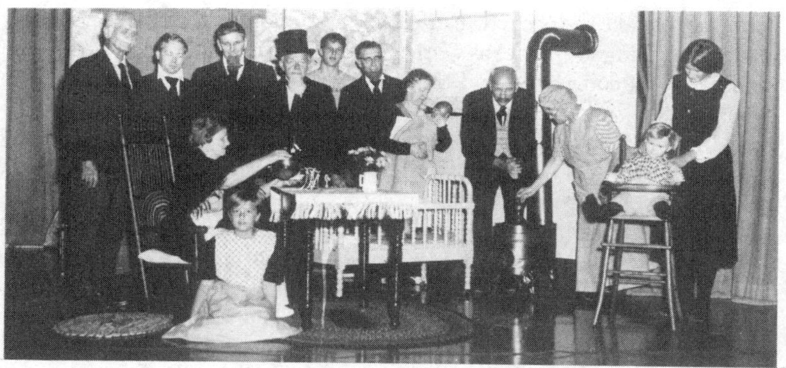

The centennial pageant, "Voices of a Century." Standing, l.-r.: Clarence Jalving, Robert Dykstra, Benjamin Plasman, the Rev. Dr. Bastian Kruithof, Thomas Bonnette, John J. Ver Beek, Bernice Mollema Dykstra, Dr. Henry Ten Pas, Irene Ver Beek, and Judith Jalving; seated at table, Elsie Jalving, and child, Mary Bruins.

husband, Bastian, wrote the script. On centennial Sunday, September 10, the former ministers, William Van't Hof, Jacob Sessler, and Christian Walvoord, participated in the worship services conducted in Dimnent Memorial Chapel of Hope College and in Hope Church. Fellowship Hall was the setting for a historical program Sunday evening, November 5, 1967. Surrounded by an exhibit of old photographs and relics of the church, the congregation viewed slides showing many scenes of former days.

The interesting events of the centennial observance marked the conclusion of one century and the entrance into the second. Although the Americanization process continued apace right up to the congregation's centennial celebration, it especially continued to provide a momentum and dynamic that gave the church renewal after World War II during the pastorates of Christian Walvoord and Russell Vande Bunte. The long Americanization process and accompanying phenomenon of "progressive characteristics" continued as vital aspects of the congregation's life. These two forces, in tandem, indicated that the church was willing to adopt new methods reflecting American life, culture, and practice without losing sight of its theological heritage and love for biblical preaching. Third Church, therefore, was in a position to face the future with an optimism that would continue to make the church an effective instrument of God in the on-going work of the Kingdom of Jesus Christ. However, once the restoration of the sanctuary was completed and the centennial celebration concluded, the congregation was confronted by changing times brought on by the acceleration of the conflict in Viet Nam, the cultural revolution of the rising hippie generation in American society, the decline of the mainline church, and the challenge to make a greater Christian social impact on society. The next twenty-five years in the history of Third Church would bring changes in the life of the congregation completely unthinkable in 1968. The Americanization process, so much lauded during the earlier years, needed to be reevaluated also. Changes would bring challenges, but challenges would be met.

The restored church, 1968.

VII
New Challenges in a Changing Era

The changing times in American national life during the late sixties and early seventies were matched by the changing patterns of church life. The influential ministry of the Rev. Dr. Billy Graham initiated a new religious awakening in American society. The precise starting point of Graham's influence in America may be traced to his summer-long crusade in New York's Madison Square Garden in 1957.[1] Protestantism reached a peak in numbers that year. A few years later, the Charismatic movement[2] under the leadership of such persons as Episcopalian rector Dennis Bennett, made itself felt in many Protestant denominations and the Roman Catholic church as well. Revivalism probably made its greatest impact in the Baptist churches of America, leading historian Martin E. Marty to comment on the "baptistification" of America.[3] The converts to the Charismatic movement swelled the membership of churches of Pentecostal-type denominations such as the Assemblies of God. Strangely enough, there was another major shift underway during the same period. Old denominational groups such as the Episcopalians, Presbyterians, United Methodists, and United Church of Christ, now referred to as mainline churches,[4] entered a period of decline; the same was true of the Reformed Church in America.

The Reformed Church in America, with which Third Reformed Church has always been affiliated, was a "mixed bag." The denomination included the churches of New York and New Jersey, many of which were organized in the seventeenth and eighteenth centuries. Yet it included the younger churches of the Midwest and far west, most of which came out of the nineteenth- and early twentieth-century German and Dutch emigrations to the United States. Many of the Dutch immigrants had come out of the 1834 Afscheiding or Separatist movement in the Netherlands under the leadership of the Rev. Hendrik de Cock.[5]

The particular challenge which Third Church faced after its centennial celebration in 1967 came because the preceding century of Americanization had brought the congregation closer to the ethos of the eastern Reformed churches than to those found generally in the Midwest. The strong influence of Pastors Henry Utterwick (1872-1880), James Martin (1920-1934), and Christian Walvoord (1950-1958) led Third Church to take on some of the characteristics of the mainline churches. This trend was furthered by the effective ministries of Robert Hoeksema (1971-1978) and Willis Jones (1979-1986), both of whom pastored eastern Reformed churches prior to serving at Third. However, just when the congregation of Third Reformed Church entered into the mainstream of American Protestant Christianity, many denominations in the mainstream entered an unfortunate period of precipitous decline.

Americanization and a progressive spirit which had seemed a great blessing suddenly caused Third Church to be confronted with an identity crisis. Following the period from 1987 to 1990, when the congregation lost 116 members during a time of ministerial leadership crisis, it was time to take stock. Had the congregation lost members because it had become mainline, or were other factors involved, such as changes in the immediate neighborhood or the competition of the megachurches which first appeared in Holland in the 1970s?

By the 125th anniversary year, which was celebrated from September, 1992, to June, 1993, the church had experienced renewal in outlook, vision, and spiritual strength, the congregation now being led by its senior pastor, the Rev. Dr. Steven S. Stam. Having become a mainline congregation, Third Church was challenged to see if there could be a change of direction so that the traditional mainline decline would be reversed. Happily, Third Church would not decline like so many mainline churches even though there was to be a loss of membership briefly in the later nineteen eighties. Decline was avoided because of the effective ministries of key pastors and many talented lay persons since the celebration of the church's centennial anniversary in

The consistory, 1967 Standing, l.-r. Carl Todd, the Rev. Russell Vande Bunte, Thomas G. Bos, Gus Feenstra, Alwin De Haan, Garrett Vander Borgh, Ronald Boven, James Prins, Arthur Tazelaar, John Paarlberg, Carl Miller, Gordon Brewer, Robert Notier, Jack Bolhuis, the Rev. Mark Walvoord, Eugene Jekel, Andrew Vollink, Leslie Van Beveren, and Donald Ihrman; seated, l.-r. Gleon Bonnette, George Stephens, Bruce Boundy, Ben Plasman, Donald Frego, Marvin Jalving, Ivan Bosman, and John VerBeek

1967. A review of the events in the life of Third Church during the past twenty-five years will provide an understanding of how Third Church met new challenges in a changing era.

New Directions in Christian Education

Pastoral leadership played a key role throughout the history of the congregation and was equally important as the congregation moved into its second century at the time of the restoration of the sanctuary and the celebration of the centennial. During his pastorate from 1959 to 1969, the Rev. Russell Vande Bunte was everything that the congregation looked for in a senior pastor. The quality of his preaching gifts, his administrative skills, and his pastoral heart were exactly what the members of the congregation expected in their senior minister. But soon after Third Church entered the second century of its history, Pastor Vande Bunte accepted a call to the First Reformed Church of Ridgewood, New Jersey. From November, 1969, to February, 1971, the pulpit of Third was "vacant," to use a traditional term. Happily for Third Reformed Church, the associate pastor, the Rev. Mark Walvoord, who had come on staff in 1967 as minister of Christian education, filled a large void in pastoral leadership at this crucial time. More importantly, he set the pattern for the direction of the Christian education program for the next couple of decades. Pastor Walvoord recognized the changes in life and society and saw the need to adopt new forms of Christian education in the congregation. The impact of his leadership in the Christian education program during his seven-year ministry was profound and established a pattern of effective Christian education in the congregation for his successors: John Paarlberg, Kathy Jo Blaske, and Karen Schakel.

In 1968, the year after Walvoord assumed his duties, a special Committee on Evaluation of the Christian Education Program recommended major changes for Third Church. The Wednesday evening Family Night program had been lagging; and because fewer and fewer members of the congregation were taking advantage of this program, it was discontinued. For children in grades one through six, a Sunday evening session of church school was inaugurated at 5 p.m., and the evening worship service moved from 7 p.m. to 5 p.m. to accommodate the new program and younger families. The youth groups were also scheduled to meet at 5 p.m., and a once-a-month family service was established for evening worshipers. The catechetical classes for grades seven through twelve continued to be held on Wednesday evenings. Congregational suppers were held quarterly at 5 p.m. on Sundays. Much of the plan was adopted. Later a Youth Club including a supper provided by the parents was organized for fourth, fifth, and sixth graders on Thursday afternoons. Although modified through the years, the Youth Club continues as a vital part of the Christian education program.

Mr. Walvoord enabled changes in adult education to take place. The popular Discussion Class considered current topics and examined contemporary religious literature. For instance, the candidates for mayor of Holland, Louis Hallacy II and L. W. Lamb, Jr., were invited into the class on March 28, 1971, to explain their views on social issues which faced the Holland community. The more usual format was the discussion of books, led by various members of the class. Many of these books were published in the new Reformed/Presbyterian curriculum, Covenant Life Curriculum, were especially interesting. This type of approach to adult Christian education ultimately led to the demise during the later 1960s and 1970s of the traditional adult Sunday school classes such as the Gleaners, Adult Bible Class, and the Fellowship Class. Though these classes had been the major vehicles for effective adult education earlier, they failed to attract the younger members of the congregation even though they had very effective teachers such as John VerBeek, a Hope College professor, and Clara Reeverts, a Holland High School teacher.

Again Walvoord found a way to counteract the decline in the attendance of the traditional adult classes. He inaugurated the "Mini-course" system for adult education. Two or three courses, each one lasting usually six weeks, were offered at the same time, thus providing a choice. This program was so well received that even the Discussion Class ran its course and disbanded. As many as 120 adults attended classes on various topics. This system's popularity has continued to the present, and many other congregations have initiated the same practice. For instance, the Rev. Darrell Franken taught

The Rev. Mark L. Walvoord, associate minister, 1967-1974

"Wholistic Health" and Jantina Holleman instructed a class in "History of Sacred Music" in 1982. Professor David Myers taught "Psychology Through the Eyes of Faith" and the Rev. Dr. Robert Palma gave lectures on Dietrich Bonhoeffer in 1988. The mini-courses were successful because almost all teachers were drawn from the ranks of college and seminary professors and talented members of the congregation.

Before Pastor Walvoord left in 1974 to become pastor of the Parkview Reformed Church in Cleveland, Ohio, he inaugurated discussion about the possibility of having the church consider the Bethel Bible Series program which had been instituted by a Lutheran pastor in Madison, Wisconsin. Eventually the program was adopted. In January, 1976, Pastors Robert Hoeksema and John Paarlberg took the leadership training course at the Bethel Bible headquarters. Paarlberg then trained study leaders in the congregation so that they could teach the Bethel Series of Bible studies to others. The Bethel Series offered serious biblical study to the adults in the

The Rev. Robert J. Hoeksema, senior minister, 1971-1978.

The Rev. John D. Paarlberg, minister of education, 1976-1978; minister of parish life, 1979-1981.

congregation. Hundreds of members of the church have gone through the program and have been greatly enriched in their knowledge of the Bible.

At the very time Mark Walvoord was constructing a creative Christian education program for the congregation, Third Church provided the home for a unique Christian education experience for children and young adults with various kinds of disabilities. This special education ministry was inaugurated in 1968 by William Paarlberg, a student at Western Seminary who attended Third Church. Third had been chosen to be the host church because "its auditory system [was] particularly suited to work with the deaf and hard-of-hearing."[6] John Brinkman, a dedicated layperson from the Maplewood Reformed Church, had suggested the program originally. The team of Marcy Vanderwel and Marti Bultman followed Paarlberg in giving the program key leadership for many years. In 1988, it was reported that forty-five children and adults received one-on-one instruction from volunteers.[7] The teaching staff has always included a number of Hope

College students. The very successful program celebrated its twenty-fifth anniversary in April, 1993.[8] Several members of Third Church also participated in the program. A prime mover has been Lynne Ihrman who provided much inspiration for the endeavor and who served on the board for many years. Her daughter, Laurel, was a student for several years and then became one of the teachers.

Christian Social Action

The social upheaval of the nineteen sixties made a major impact on American society, especially through the Civil Rights movement. The revolution also made an impact on American church life. Moderate Protestant churches like Third Reformed Church had some sensitivity to social issues, but the social dimension of the gospel was often hampered by a misunderstanding of the Social Gospel Movement which had made a great impact on American churches earlier in the century. The Social Gospel Movement, for which Walter Rauschenbusch provided major inspiration, based its work on liberal theology which was anathema among conservative Protestants. For example, liberal theologians did not consider the virgin birth of Jesus Christ or his bodily resurrection vital beliefs, as was noted in chapter five. But the aversion to forthright Christian social action was largely overcome in many denominations such as the Reformed Church in America through the founding of national denominational commissions which studied ways in which churches could meet the needs of American society.

The impulse for better Christian social action programs was felt in Third Church by the time of the celebration of its centennial in 1967. In 1969, the congregation joined neighboring churches and organizations in a local organization called Churches United for Social Action (CUSA). Dale Van Lente, a leading layperson and prominent businessman, represented Third Church and was elected treasurer of the steering committee. This committee of thirteen persons established the Community Action House as a nonprofit organization. Hope College loaned the new organization a home for use as headquarters on East 8th Street. When that building had to be vacated for the construction of the new Holland post office, the organization moved to West 14th Street. The Community Action House plays a vital role in the life of the Holland community, meeting the needs of disadvantaged residents of the city. Several members of Third Church have served on the board.[9]

In early 1970, Third Church became the home of a branch of the day care center which had been started March 23, 1966, for fifteen children in the Hope Reformed Church. When more space was needed, Margaret Steffens and Nell Wichers established a branch of the center at Third Church. Mrs. Wichers was vice president of the board of directors as well. Another Christian social service organization, the Good Samaritan Center, was organized in Holland in the late sixties, and Third Church members have been involved in its founding, support, and governance.[10]

Some members of the congregation, wanting to build on the growing interest in Christian social action, petitioned the consistory May 4, 1970, to form a Christian Action Council. Consistory responded quickly and the council held its first meeting on May 11. The first chairperson reported to the consistory December 11, 1972, on the nature of its work.[11] The council investigated many avenues of Christian service available to the community and urged the congregation to support many of them. Through the council, Third Church began to support a wide range of Christian organizations actively engaged in service to the community. For instance, the council reported in 1986 that Third Church was financially supporting the Holland Area Child Development Services, the Christian Counseling Service, Child and Family Services, Higher Horizons (a youth program at Hope College), Ottagan Alcoholic Rehabilitation, Good Samaritan Center, Community Action House, Women in Transition, and Hospice of Holland.[12] Interest in these organizations by Third Church also led to the participation of many of its members as volunteers in these local organizations.

The work of the council and the inspiration created by Christian action led to many other significant projects during the past quarter century. Carol Westphal organized a "Simpler Lifestyles Workshop" which was held October 6, 1979. Karin and Wesley Granberg-Michaelson were the keynote speakers. "Live simply so that others may simply live" was the pervasive theme of this thought-provoking and spiritually stimulating conference. Through the efforts of Betty Lou Voskuil, great interest in world hunger awareness was generated in the congregation. She and Mary De Young recruited 116 Third Church persons to participate in the CROP walk April 16, 1983.[13] In 1984, there were 113 walkers who raised $4,356 for that worthy cause.[14] Third often had the highest number of participants in this annual event, which continues to generate much interest each spring in the Holland community. In 1983, Mrs. Voskuil became the Hunger Associate for the Reformed Church in America and was also invited to serve on the national board of Bread for the World.

The inauguration of the Stephen Series in 1980 under the leadership of the associate pastor, John Paarlberg, also reflected greater diaconal sensitivity on the part of the congregation. Paarlberg noted in an editorial in the May, 1980, *Newsletter* that "...through the Stephen Series system of training and organization, we will be developing a workable and lasting program of caring ministry." The associate pastor went to a two-week training course in St. Louis, Missouri, August 3 through 15 in order to implement the program in Third Church. When the course for this vital lay ministry was instituted, he also noted that "...this [fifty hours of] training will include such topics as how to listen effectively, how to deal with feelings, how to use the traditional resources of Christianity in helping, how to maintain confidentiality, how to help persons experiencing crises, and many other areas of concern." The first class of Stephen ministers, consisting of fourteen members, was commissioned Sunday, May 17, 1981.[15] The associate pastors continue to have the responsibility of carrying out this very effective program, and many members of the congregation have gone through the local training.

Undoubtedly the growing interest in Christian social concerns was also instrumental in the very successful Annville project in 1983. Reformed Church North American Mission funds had supported the Annville Institute in Kentucky for years, and the very name, Annville, meant an opportunity for service. Pastor Willis Jones proposed in the fall of 1982 that the church assume the entire responsibility for the summer program of the Annville Institute during July and August of 1983. All publicity, program, and personnel would be provided by Third Church including, of course, all funding. Personnel would fill the responsibilities of "cooks, dining hall workers, canteen operator, pool worker and manager, work camp supervisors, retreat workers, gardeners, groundskeepers, Bible School workers, and whatever else happens to fit into the program!"[16] A steering committee was formed under the leadership of John Hutchinson and Graham Duryee. The dates for this project for Jackson County Ministries in Annville were set for June 18 through August 13. The project engendered considerable enthusiasm in the congregation. John Hutchinson reported in the October, 1983, issue of the church newsletter, the *Third Generation*, that 176 persons went to serve in Annville at least a week that summer and that nearly $23,000 was contributed to fund the project, which cost $24,638.96. The enthusiasm for this project propelled the congregation to undertake a similar project in The United Reformed Church, an inner city congregation in Jersey City, New Jersey, in 1986. Dr. Lars Granberg and Kris De Pree chaired the steering committee of this project.[17]

The momentum of such projects continued in the Summer of Service or "S.O.S." opportunities inaugurated in 1991 by the interim pastor, the Rev. Dr. Dennis Voskuil.[18] Under the leadership of Jane Armstrong and Steven De Young, many volunteers worked to renovate a home near the church, support the child care and social needs of migrants north of Holland, carry out another Appalachian project, and assist in giving home repair assistance to a family in New Era, Michigan. In 1992, the New Era project was to "raise" a new home for a needy family.[19] Other people who were supervised by El Slenk and Ed Ratering helped in the Housing Opportunities Made Equal (H.O.M.E.) program, which has accomplished much for people in need of adequate housing. Several members have offered assistance in the "Project Home Again" program of the Good Samaritan Center. Third was a church partner to "help find permanent housing, employment, and a more secure lifestyle" for a Holland family.[20]

During the past quarter century, Christian social action became a vital part of the life of Third Church. Hundreds of members have been personally involved in a great variety of programs, through service on the boards of the organizations and through considerable financial support. Located in the Historic District of Holland, Third Church has come to recognize that it must serve the people in the general area surrounding the church as well as the larger Holland community.

Music in the Church

The important place of music in the church has been noted in chapter two. In the very early years, the Van Lente choir was given a home at Third Church when the place of choirs was very much disputed in the Dutch-immigrant churches. Not only were choirs suspect but also the singing of any music by the congregation except the Psalms. Third Church quickly accepted the importance of the church choir and English/American hymnody. Under the leadership of John Vander Sluis, director for thirty years (1893-1923), the role of the church choir rose to new heights. Following Vander Sluis, the

The junior choir, 1968 Front row, l.-r. Mary Tazelaar, Mary Stepp, Kathy Kuiper, Jane Leenhouts, Barbara Lievense, Jane Buter, and Deborah Muir; second row, l.-r. James Voogd, John Miller, Thomas TerHaar, Dale Koeman, Peter Boven, Jon Rietberg, Stephen Bonnette, and Peter Elliot; third row, l.-r. Margery Boven, Mary Bruins, Julie Rhodes, Mark Kouw, James Paul, John Bonnette, Jeffrey Gargano; fourth row, l.-r. Laurel Ihrman, Merry Kouw, Jan Frissel, Susan Lievense, Jane Jalving, Dorothea Megow, and Jane Elliott

tenure of choir directors until 1950 was relatively short (See Appendix 10).

This changed with the appointment of Roger Rietberg as choir director and organist in 1950. His capable and vigorous leadership totaled forty-three years by the time the 125th anniversary was celebrated. His impact and influence during these years are immeasurable. A graduate of the School of Sacred Music at Union Theological Seminary in New York City, he was the first professionally trained organist and choirmaster employed by

Third Church. As professor of music during a long career at Hope College, he was in touch with the finest in choral and organ literature. Fortunately, he served a congregation which had been prepared for good church music by his predecessors. Thelma Leenhouts, in her tribute to Rietberg at the fortieth anniversary recognition of his service to Third Church on September 16, 1990, succinctly summarized his contribution by saying, "Roger, as is well known, led us and sometimes dragged us into a meaningful musical worship of God. It can also be said that the primary attraction of visitors to Third Church, who became members, was often due to the sacred music program offered under his leadership."[21]

Regular features Rietberg introduced were the Christmas Eve carol service, the annual Advent choir program, and the Tenebrae service during Holy Week. Another important feature was the bringing in of specialists in church music such as hymnwriter Brian Wren. Eric Routley, a prominent British hymnologist, called Wren "the most successful English hymn writer since Charles Wesley."[22] Dr. Wren visited Third Church in June of 1986 and again in October of 1987. At the latter appearance, Wren conducted a hymnfest. The Rietberg family commissioned him to write a children's hymn in memory of their son, Tommy, and this composition was introduced to the congregation on November 4, 1990. Wren, who contributed nine hymns to *Rejoice in the Lord*, was also commissioned to write a hymn for the 125th anniversary of the congregation in 1992-93. This hymn was introduced to the congregation when Wren again visited Third Church Sunday, April 18, 1993. Since the hymn has a very special significance for Third Church, it is reproduced in Appendix 17.

Undoubtedly this gifted hymn writer was willing to come to Third Church because of his respect for Roger Rietberg, who is widely recognized for his knowledge of hymnody. Because of Rietberg's expertise, the Reformed Church in America invited him to serve on the hymnbook committee organized in the early nineteen eighties. The Rev. Dr. Norman J. Kansfield, a member of Third Church at that time and recognized for his understanding of good church music, joined Rietberg and four other persons who engaged Eric Routley to produce a new hymnal. Mildred W. Schuppert, a member of Third Church and longtime librarian at Western Theological Seminary, provided all indices.[23] The new hymnbook, *Rejoice in the Lord*, was published in 1985. On September 8, Third Church dedicated the new hymnbooks in memory of Clarence Klaasen. The hymnbook was given critical acclaim by many persons who were experts in church music. Third's congregation has come to appreciate this hymnbook for some of the new hymns which have been learned.[24] Roger Rietberg also gave leadership in obtaining a new church organ. The Austin organ which had been installed in 1928 was showing its limitations after nearly fifty years of use. At the suggestion of the worship committee, an organ committee was appointed and led by Dr. Lars Granberg.[25] The committee made its first report in the congregational newsletter in June of 1977, and said:

> Third Church's reputation for leadership in its liturgy and music is widespread and should not only be maintained but enhanced....A new Organ would help us to continue in this ministry and help to further this rich tradition.

The congregation accepted the idea that a new organ was needed and the committee began years of arduous study and work. One major idea for consideration was placement of the organ in the balcony instead of its usual place in the chancel. A new instrument of any size needed much more room than that offered by the chancel. Robert Sipe, of Dallas, Texas, was chosen as the builder. Jon Bechtel and Paul DeMaagd, engineers by profession, supervised the installation of the new instrument because the balcony floor had to be strengthened with steel beams to support the large instrument. The placement of the new organ in the balcony also forced another change in the life of the church: adoption of two morning services. With the balcony reserved solely for the organ and choir members, a great deal of general seating was lost. Two services, already inaugurated to accommodate the worshipers,[26] were now necessary.

The cost of the new organ and related renovations was approximately $225,000. The new Sipe organ with its three manuals and thirty-four stops was dedicated Sunday, September 19, 1982, in a morning worship service.[27] Gerre Hancock, organmaster at St. Thomas Episcopal Church, New York City, played the dedicatory concert on November 14. In 1990, a Trompette-en-Chamade and more stops for the pedal were installed. During the course of the long period of time it took for the planning and purchase of the new organ, concern was expressed by some members of the congregation that it would be better to support current social needs than purchase such an expensive instrument. The congregation, although much more aware of social needs, regarded the purchase of the new organ as an important

The Sipe Organ

move.[28] The 1928 Austin organ remained in the chancel but the pipes had to be removed when the sanctuary was air conditioned in 1988. The David Skinner Organ Company purchased the console and assorted pipes and reconditioned them for later sale. The new organ, the placement of the choir in the balcony, and the skill of Rietberg as choirmaster and organist have enhanced congregational singing. The debt for the new organ was retired quickly.

It was clear that the great majority of the members of the congregation enjoyed the quality of music for worship at Third Church. Indeed, many people joined the congregation because of Third's leadership in church music. Third Church reiterated its concern for good church music when a new mission statement was presented to the congregation for consideration on June 11, 1989:

> we will emphasize the Biblically grounded preaching of God's word within worship services which are liturgically in harmony with Reformed theology and *high artistic standards* [italics mine].

It was clear that Rietberg's leadership in church music had made a great impact on the congregation.

However, when addressing the consistory at a retreat on January 13, 1990, the Rev. Robert Bast, minister of evangelism in the Reformed Church in America, expressed the opinion that a music program such as in Third Church appeals to the small percentage of the American population who like classical music. Bast suggested that the type of music appreciated by a large majority at Third Church also could be a limiting factor in attracting new members. When a survey of the congregation was made for master planning purposes in 1991, it became clear that some members of the church in the 30- to 45-year age group desired a broader range of church music. Musical tastes were shifting in the Holland Reformed churches and possibly at Third as well. New forms of church music were being introduced. So-called "praise music" was adopted by several congregations in Holland

Mildred W. Schuppert receiving recognition as an organist of Third Church in 1980 l.-r. John VerBeek, Schuppert, Jantina Holleman, and the Rev. John Paarlberg

churches. Goal #1 of the MasterPlan[29] adopted by consistory on June 9, 1992 stated:

> Provide opportunities for worship which encourage participation, recognize and value the diversity of our members, and maintain a unity of spirit. Action A: Affirm the value of our existing worship program including: ...2. Excellence in music; and ...Continue to expand the breadth of music and worship forms;....

The challenge facing the congregation will be to decide just what niche the congregation will choose to fill musically in the life of Holland, Michigan, Reformed church life.

Two Progressive Pastorates

Many challenges of the past quarter century were succcessfully met, due primarily to the leadership of two key senior pastors, the Rev. Robert Hoeksema (1971-78) and the Rev. Willis Jones (1979-86). Both made significant contributions to the life of Third Reformed Church by their ability to help the church accept new challenges and make beneficial innovations in the program of church life. Hoeksema's special gifts were in the area of administration and pastoral care, Jones's in preaching and innovative programs.

When Pastor Hoeksema assumed the position of senior minister in February, 1971, there were two church councils in existence. The Christian Education Council had been a valuable board since 1938. The Christian Action Council had just gotten underway in 1970. Hoeksema built on the council idea by forming three new councils: Evangelism, Worship, and Reception/Fellowship/Visitation. The basic structure of Third Church's life has followed along council lines. The councils study and promote the basic ideas for effective administration of the parish. Through the years, councils have been modified, merged, or renamed, but the essential pattern remains the same.

Hoeksema also emphasized the importance of professional staff. After the death of the associate minister, the Rev. Jerry A. Veldman, in 1962, Pastor Vande Bunte was the sole professional staff person along with Adelaide Veldman, who was the church secretary and, informally, the director of Christian education. The congregation finally realized in 1966 that more staff was necessary and urged the hiring of a professional Christian education director, the Rev. Mark Walvoord (who has been mentioned earlier for the success of his work). Walvoord served as an associate pastor as well, although that was not part of his title.

When Walvoord left Third Church for another pastorate in 1974, he was succeeded by the Rev. John Paarlberg in 1976. By this time, it was apparent to Rev. Hoeksema that a third fulltime staff person was necessary. Thus Kathy Jo Blaske was engaged as director of Christian education in 1978 upon her graduation from Western Theological Seminary, and Paarlberg became minister of parish life. Through Pastor Hoeksema's leadership, Third Church was awakening to the fact that in the rising consumer mentality of the public, it was necessary to offer more programming, which in turn called for more professional staff. Christ Memorial Reformed Church, then rising to prominence on the southwest side of the city, had been leading the way in this new discovery in Holland church life, and many of the other churches in the city were also developing multiple staffs. By the time Mr. Hoeksema accepted a call to the Addisville Reformed Church, Richboro, Pennsylvania, in the fall of 1978, Third Church was fully staffed and doing well in all aspects of church life.

Robert Hoeksema was also pastor of Third Church at a crucial time during the debate in the denomination over the ordination of women, first to the offices of elder and deacon and then to the pastoral ministry. The Reformed Church in America opened the offices of elder and deacon to women in 1972.[30] The congregation was prepared to move deliberately in this matter, although many congregations in the denomination were opposed to what was then considered a radical change in church life. Third Church opened the offices to women the following year. Jantina Holleman was elected the first woman elder December 9, 1973, and was ordained January 6, 1974. On December 8, 1974, Erma Bruggink was elected elder. On February 8, 1976, Phyllis De Haan was the first woman to be elected deacon. In a short time, other very capable women such as Etta Hesselink, Elaine Tanis, Carol Gargano, and Elaine Jekel became members of the consistory and Jekel was elected the first woman vice-president of consistory in January of 1979. Women in Third Church were finally recognized for their gifts beyond the traditional women's roles that had existed since 1867 in the congregation. The congregation was pleased when one of its elders, Dr. Beth Marcus, was elected the first woman president of the General Synod of the Reformed Church in America in 1992.

Although the role of women was greatly enlarged at Third Church in the nineteen seventies, women members continued to enrich the life of the congregation through their more traditional roles as well. The organization Reformed Church Women, or RCW for short, was the focal point of women's ministries at Third. The annual program booklets of RCW indicate that among the activities of members included fund-raisers such as baking birthday cakes for Hope College students, serving Tulip Time meals, and making apple dumplings; participating in the Western Seminary Women's Auxiliary; and arranging receptions for special occasions. Their giving for benevolent causes augmented the church's outreach ministry. Members of the circles meet monthly for Bible study, fellowship, and business. Each circle is responsible for some of the shut-ins. The quietness of RCW members' good deeds do not veil the indispensability of their vital service at Third Church.[31]

Kathy Jo Blaske, director of Christian education since 1978, became one of the first beneficaries of the change in interpretation of the Book of Church Order of the Reformed Church in America that permitted the

The Rev. Kathy Jo Blaske, minister of education, 1978-1988

ordination of women to the pulpit ministry.[32] On August 14, 1979, the consistory called her as minister by a vote of 27 to 1. She was ordained and installed on October 28. Because of that step in 1979, accepting a woman minister simply was not an issue when the Pastoral Search Committee recommended in 1993 that the Rev. Kathryn Davelaar be called as associate pastor. Women finally entered fully into all aspects of Third Church's life by the conclusion of the Hoeksema pastorate.

Hoeksema introduced some very good program ideas. "A Family Affair," a denominational lay witness program, was conducted March 23 to 25, 1973.[33] An elaborate workshop was held involving many members of the congregation. Another well-received program included weekends with outstanding guest preachers. The Rev. Dr. Leonard A. Griffith of Toronto, Canada, conducted a workshop on church life and preaching November 14-16, 1975. The Rev. and Mrs. Gordon Cosby of the Church of the Savior in Washington, D.C., spent an enriching weekend with the congregation at Third in the fall of 1976. The Rev. Dr. Bruce Thieleman, Dean of the Chapel at Grove City College, Pennsylvania, was the guest preacher October 27-29, 1978. The members of Third enjoyed the masterful sermons preached by each of the guests.

A Religious Arts Festival was held March 13-14, 1976, the first of its kind for Third Church. Etta Hesselink and her committee provided a valuable experience for the congregation to "explore ways in which the arts can express and contribute to the life and worship of a Christian congregation."[34] Workshops demonstrated woodblock technique, banner making, creative sacred dance, and decoupage. This festival encouraged Pastor Hoeksema and Mr. Rietberg to add a greater sense of celebration to the worship services. A sacred dance group, many of whose members were also members at Third, enhanced worship services periodically. Third Church also received a gift of handbells from Henry DuMez and Mabel DuMez Frei in 1976.[35] Two bell choirs formed by Evelyn Rietberg have contributed much to worship services and their celebrative nature.

Hoeksema's high sense of worship enabled him to offer moving pastoral prayers in worship services. His pastoral sensitivity also drew a large number of new people to Third Church during his pastorate, averaging more than fifty people a year for a total of 418. Because of his openness and love for people, Mr. Hoeksema was also able to bring into membership people of all social classes in the community.

Crystal Walvoord leading the singing of the children in a Family Affair event, 1973

Happily for Third Church, Pastor Willis Jones was equally skilled in leading the congregation to accept new challenges. Several members enjoyed discussing theological writings in the Guild for Lay Theologians which he led. Mr. Jones initiated the very successful Annville and Jersey City projects described above. The Dublin, Ohio, project was a church planting near Columbus in 1984. This project was greatly aided by members of Third Church who provided funds and served as volunteers and, in a sense, as professional staff.[36] Jean Boven Norden, wife of the founding pastor, the Rev. Stephen Norden, grew up in Third Church. The Nordens' strong leadership enabled this church planting to be a very successful venture.

Jones, who specialized in the area of worship, received a Doctor of Ministry degree from Western Theological Seminary with an emphasis on worship while serving at Third. The congregation appreciated his exceptional preaching skills. He developed a reputation as a great pulpiteer, and during his pastorate 495 men, women, and children were added to the congregation. He also restructured the annual confirmation class procedures and assisted many young people in the development of their Christian faith during his ministry. A crucial change introduced by Pastor Jones was to drop the evening service, which had come to be very poorly attended, and to institute "Kerk Night" in its place during the fall of 1984.[37] A varied program of opportunities was offered, including Bible study for adults, Bethel Bible classes, the Stephen Series, the Junior and Senior High Youth Fellowship meetings, a vesper service in the chancel, and evening church school. This program enabled the church to continue the evening service in a new format.

Since Willis Jones had an ability to understand the distinctive nature of Third Church, he was able to guide the congregation effectively. His description of the congregation was printed in the September, 1984, newsletter. It is worth quoting in full because it indicates how well Pastor Jones had his finger on the pulse of the congregation:

The Rev. Dr. Willis A. Jones, senior minister, 1979-1986

> [Third Church members] are conservative in theology, while progressive in ethics; they are pious in the best sense of the word, but also worldly in the best sense of the word. They themselves are strong and possessed by a strong sense of identity; but yet, see themselves richly blessed in order to become a blessing. They exalt good liturgy, good preaching, good music, but they also genuinely struggle with the requirements of outreach, benevolence and neighborhood involvement. They want to be fed within, but they also seek to minister without. They honor their own traditions, but warmly embrace others than their own. They love the church and are committed to it; but they know they are also required to minister to the larger community. They know the requirements of discipleship, while enjoying the prerequisites of a humane and gracious life. They permit and encourage their membership both to pray and to play. They are restrained in their emotions, yet genuine in their deeds of quiet compassion and servanthood....[38]

The congregation was reluctant to see their pastor accept a call to the Wyckoff Reformed Church of Wyckoff, New Jersey, in 1986. Since he was so highly regarded for his preaching skills and possessed such an infectious good humor, everyone, in gratitude for his ministry, said, "Amen," after the enthusiastic "Alleluia" Pastor Jones spoke at the conclusion of morning worship. The combination of the successful pastorates of Hoeksema and Jones had brought another "splendid" period into the life of Third Church.

But times would quickly change. A profound change was occurring in the church life of Holland, Michigan, which made an impact on virtually all the churches of the community including Third Reformed Church. The megachurch concept had arrived in Holland. For decades, there had been large congregations in the United States. Roman Catholic church parishes, for example, often were very large. For years Third's neighbor, St. Francis de Sales Roman Catholic Church, had some 3,000 members. However, the megachurch as a concept in American Protestantism began to influence church life in Holland, through the examples of two congregations in particular: the Crystal Cathedral, a Reformed Church in America congregation founded by a Hope College and Western Theological Seminary graduate, the Rev. Dr. Robert H. Schuller, and the 15,000 member Willow Creek Church in suburban Chicago, founded by William Hybels, who grew up in the Christian Reformed church in Kalamazoo. Both these megacongregations have been widely noted in the media.

During the successful pastorates of Pastors Hoeksema and Jones, two Holland congregations were developing into very large if not "megachurches," thereby setting styles of worship and church life for other churches in the city. The Rev. Paul Hontz participated in leading a relatively small Central Wesleyan Church, situated at the corner of 17th Street and Pine Avenue, into a megachurch congregation, now located on West Fortieth Street; and the Rev. Ronald Beyer in 1970 guided Christ Memorial Reformed Church toward megachurch status, thus influencing greatly the Reformed churches in the Holland community. Prior to Beyer's ministry, Christ Memorial, founded in 1957, was a typical Reformed church congregation. With Beyer's coming, Christ Memorial began to grow very rapidly. His innovative ideas combined with his charismatic personality to attract many members from other churches, Third included. Even though the successful pastorate of Hoeksema prevented any considerable slippage of membership at Third

The Rev. Harold M. Delhagen (minister of parish life, 1982-1985) with Donna and Kyle Delhagen.

Church, the congregation began to lose net membership by 1984, when the ministry of Willis Jones was at its zenith.

There is always some loss of membership in a congregation like Third, because people move elsewhere and transfer membership or lose interest and drop their memberships. However, by the time Jones left in 1986, the loss of members to Christ Memorial (though not to Central Wesleyan) had reached considerable proportions. The innovative leadership of Mr. Beyer and his successors, particularly the Rev. Dr. Timothy Brown, enabled Christ Memorial to grow from 636 men, women, and children (as reported in the 1971 General Synod statistics) to 2,425 by the end of 1986. In 1994, the total membership of Christ Memorial Reformed Church exceeded 3,000. A total of ninety persons of Third united with that congregation between 1970 and 1993.[39] With the loss of that many members to one neighboring Reformed congregation, Third Church became painfully aware that there was a new player in the competitive church life of Holland, Michigan.

The Rev. Ronald M. Franklyn, associate minister, 1986-1991

The Roorda Pastorate

With the arrival in 1987 of a new senior pastor, the Rev. Ervin Roorda, Third Church was entering a critical period in its existence in spite of all the appearances to the contrary. Roorda had been raised in the Reformed Church in America and was a graduate of Central College and Western Theological Seminary, but he had transferred to the United Presbyterian denomination after his first parish in the denomination. While Willis Jones had noted that Third held a tension within itself between traditional and contemporary attitudes, Pastor Roorda, who had served several Presbyterian pastorates successfully, apparently considered Third to be a mainline congregation like the church he had served previously in Spokane, Washington. He developed his program accordingly. He correctly noted that the longtime Americanization process which had given Third progressive characteristics placed Third Reformed Church in the typical mainline stance. For instance, the traditional evening service was discontinued; the innovations of Willis Jones for Sunday evening fell by the wayside; there no longer was Sunday school during the summer; the formal catechetical program had been discontinued decades earlier along with the traditional Wednesday evening Family Night program. The total membership of the church including men, women, and children numbered over 1,000 persons, but attendance at worship was often not far above 400 and sometimes fell below that number. Despite the creativity of the pastors and staff at Third in developing new programs, Third had apparently entered fully the mainline stream along with Hope Reformed Church of Holland before it, both of which differed in character from the other Reformed churches in the Holland Classis.

Third's membership losses raised the frightening possibility that it was going in the same direction as the major mainline churches: decline. A headline in *Newsweek* magazine, December 22, 1986, read: "From Mainline to Sideline: once the religious establishment, liberal Protestants are losing their sheep." *Time* magazine said on May 27, 1989: "Those Mainline Blues: America's old guard Protestant churches confront unprecedented decline." Like many Presbyterian, Methodist, and Episcopalian congregations, Third Church seemed to be going in the same direction. Some key members in the congregation began to question the current style of ministry. The consistory was concerned, and the elders took action. After a three-year period from

The Rev. Dr. Ervin G. Roorda with parishioner, Derek Voskuil

1987 to 1990 when membership decline amounted to 116 persons, Pastor Roorda's style and quality of ministerial leadership were questioned.[40] Under the circumstances, Pastor Roorda decided he could not continue as Third's pastor.

After Roorda's resignation took effect at the end of February of 1990, the congregation had to take stock of itself and determine the direction in which it wanted to go. The painful process of re-evaluation began under the leadership of the Rev. Gordon Timmerman, a church consultant who specialized in conflict resolution. This unsettling period negatively impacted the ministry of the able associate pastor, the Rev. Ronald Franklyn, who left in 1991 to accept a call to the Pequannock Reformed Church, Wayne, New Jersey.

A member of the congregation, the Rev. Dr. Dennis N. Voskuil, a highly respected professor of religion at Hope College and a Reformed church minister with considerable preaching and pastoral skills, agreed to serve as interim minister from 1990 to 1992, taking temporary leave from his duties at Hope College. Much of the pain experienced by the congregation ended during his brief but effective ministry. His calling program and ministry with the young adults were highlights of his devoted service to Third Church. His openness and warm personality made him a much loved pastor. During his brief ministry, the position of coordinator of pastoral care was instituted and Delores Bechtel was recruited to provide a closer bond among the members of the congregation. Third Church also embarked on a major master planning process that set the vision for the congregation into the 21st century. By the time the process was concluded, the new senior minister, the Rev. Dr. Steven S. Stam, had been installed (August 23, 1992), and the congregation was ready to move forward with renewed vigor and enthusiasm.

Administration/Laity/Building Plans

The administration of church life during recent decades followed essentially the administrative pattern set by Christian Walvoord in the 1950s, as

The Rev. Dr. Dennis N. Voskuil, acting senior minister, 1990-1992

reported in chapter six. With the appointments of Mark Walvoord and his successor, John Paarlberg, the associate pastor covered the fields of Christian education and pastoral care. When Kathy Jo Blaske became the third staff person, her major responsibility was Christian education while Paarlberg assumed the task of congregational care. Associate Pastor Harold Delhagen (1982-1985) who succeeded him, Ronald Franklyn (1986-91), and Kathryn Davelaar (1993-) assumed much of the responsibility for pastoral care, the Stephen Ministries program, and senior citizens.

A significant development in the professional leadership of the congregation has been the hiring of nonordained persons. Karen Schakel succeeded Blaske in the field of Christian education. She was given the major responsibility of church administration also. With her appointment to this important aspect of church life, the pastors have been relieved of much of the administrative detail that goes with pastoral leadership. Professional youth leaders have also become part of the Third Church staff. Todd Van Grouw (1987-90), Kevin Hart (1990-92), and Paul Beauchamp (1992-) have been responsible for this area of church life. Beauchamp pioneered a new role in that Third Church entered into partnership with the nationally recognized Young Life program. The youth minister heads up all youth programs at Third Church and also works in the Young Life program in Holland High School. A third lay person mentioned earlier, Delores Bechtel, serves as coordinator of pastoral care.

The contribution of the laity to the life of the church anywhere is taken for granted. It is no different at Third Church, where the laity has developed a tradition for significant contributions to the work of the congregation. The roots of this valuable heritage may well go back to Isaac Cappon, a key lay leader who inaugurated and superintended the Sunday school work at Third in 1867, and to his successor, the attorney Arend Visscher. The names of the multitude of laypersons who gave great service to the church are listed in the appendices. Elders, deacons, music directors, presidents of the women's groups, Sunday school superintendents, and others in major lay roles are noted.

Certain programs during the last quarter century have been successful due to the leadership of many dedicated members of the congregation. While Third Church has placed great emphasis upon the necessity of calling qualified ordained leadership, it must not be overlooked that particular programs have been successful because of the leadership exercised by the laity. One such program has been the development of the nursery program and children's worship. After the restoration of the sanctuary was completed in 1968, a new nursery program was introduced by Erma Bruggink, Barbara Brink, and Libby Boven. New nursery rooms were constructed in the area beneath the sanctuary during the 1967-68 church year. These women had a vision for a program that would be more than just child care during the morning worship service. At the time the new Covenant Life Curriculum was being introduced in the Reformed Church in America, and the Classis of Holland offered training sessions for nursery attendants. A planned curriculum was then put in place changing child care into an educational venture.[41]

The Children and Worship program is another example of a lay-inspired, lay-led venture. It has supplanted the Junior Church service instituted by Christian Walvoord shortly after he began his ministry at Third Church. This new movement for children was conceived and pioneered by Dr. Sonja Stewart, professor of Christian education at Western Theological Seminary in 1986.[42] Collette De Nooyer, a member of Third Church during the later eighties and a graduate of Western Seminary with a degree in Christian education, helped develop this model of worship for children. Third Church entered the program during Advent of 1987, when Kathy Jo Blaske, Jane Cronkite, and Alice Vogel served as worship leaders. When Blaske left for another position, Cronkite and Vogel were the principal leaders by September of 1988.[43] The Children's Worship Center provides a vital worship opportunity for young children and is staffed by trained, capable lay leaders.

The Inter-Parish Council, organized by Willis Jones in 1983, proved to be the means by which some members of Third Church have been able to carry out meaningful service to the people in the near west side of Holland where Third Church is located. St. Francis de Sales and First United Methodist churches were partners in this venture. The success of the council can be attributed primarily to laypersons who discovered that the program of the council provided a significant means by which people in the neighborhood of these three core city congregations could be served more adequately. Several other churches later joined the council.[44] For several years, the council sponsored the "Fiesta Feest [sic]." In November, 1983, a Kid's Club was formed as a weekly activity for neighborhood children during after-school hours by Alice Vogel. In a concern for the older youth, a task force of council members established the Holland Area Youth Center Advocacy

Board. This led to the organization of the Boys and Girls Club of Holland. Greg Veenstra, Donald Ihrman, and Elly Muiderman were members of the task force, with Feenstra and Muiderman becoming members of board when the club was organized.[45] Numerous other projects were initiated by the Inter-Parish Council.

Members of the Christian Action Council proposed in 1981 that Third Church offer assistance to a refugee family from Southeast Asia.[46] Following Consistory approval, Third Church received the Chang family from Cambodia into its midst. The family had been in Thailand since October 10, 1979, waiting for an American sponsor. Yun An and Chin Chy Chang came during the fall of 1981 with their children, three daughters, aged 13, 12, and 10, and two sons, 8 and 6. Their names were, respectively, Py Ing, Chun Hor, Seav Ing, Seav E, and Seave Won. LaVerne Lievense was chair of the committee which made all the arrangements to provide a home, work, and hospitality for this family. The Changs, Roman Catholic by faith, were bakers by trade.

Members of the church staff, 1994: l.-r. Delores Bechtel, the Rev. Kathryn Davelaar, the Rev. Dr. Steven S. Stam, Karen Schakel, Paul Beauchamp, Roger Rietberg, and Evelyn Rietberg

Members of the church staff, 1994: l.-r. Judy Bosch, Lynnae Schoon, James VerHulst, Carol TerBeek, and Ann Van Ingen

The dramatic story of the escape of the Changs from Communist domination appeared in the May, 1982, *Third Generation*. The Changs were given a heartfelt farewell when they moved to Palm Springs, California, where they have established a very successful business.[47]

One more example of successful and vital lay leadership is the building program inaugurated after the master plan was concluded. Goal number eight of the plan declared: [that the congregation] provide a functional, flexible, welcoming and pleasant facility which enables us to achieve our goals [one through seven] and provide an appropriate and adequate setting for our programs in a manner which preserves the historical significance of the structure.[48] Douglas Walvoord assumed overall chairmanship of the committees to formulate plans for the replacement of the entire parish hall addition, which was constructed in the early 1950s during the pastorate of Chris Walvoord. Mark Bonnette contributed his architectural knowledge to the $3,500,000 proposal for modern facilities to provide the space for the many programs of inreach and outreach of the congregation. The

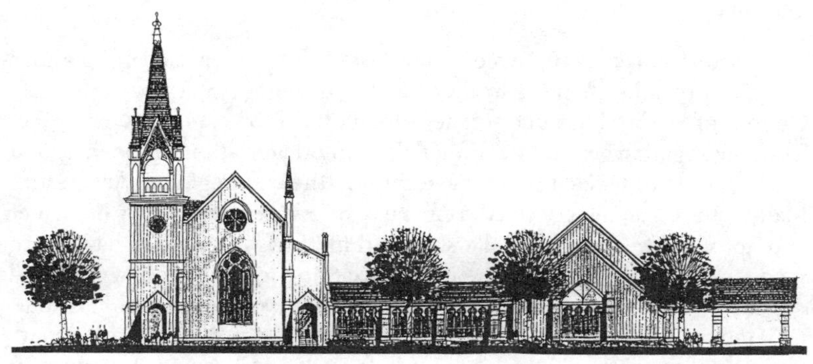

A sketch of the new parish hall addition, 1995

congregation gave tentative approval to the plans at a meeting on April 17, 1994, when a major funds campaign was approved, a campaign under the supervision of Harold Ritsema, a member of the development staff of Western Theological Seminary and a member of the congregation. On May 15, the congregation gave the green light to this major program. The members of Third Church realize, as one member[49] said, "Unless we expand and improve our facilities, we will be unable to carry out our mission into the 21st century." Another member stated that "...we must compete [with successful churches in Holland] or Third church as we know it and love it will die with us." [50]

These were strong words, but the sentiments were shared by the majority of Third's members. A successful fund raising campaign resulted in gifts and pledges amounting approximately to $1,500,000. On November 6, 1994, the congregation vacated the entire premises for a year in preparation for the demolition of the parish hall facilities and for the construction of a whole new addition to the historic sanctuary, which had been dedicated 120 years before that very month. Hope College and Western Theological Seminary graciously loaned the congregation the use of their facilities during the full year of construction. The beautiful facility was completed in the fall of 1995. Its exterior matched the carpenter Gothic of the historic sanctuary. The yellow brick exterior of the former addition was eliminated. The old and new parts of Third Church now appeared as one.

The Americanization Theme Revisited

The word and concept, "Americanization,"[51] have been used in a popular sense in previous chapters to describe the changes the Third Reformed Church of Holland has undergone through the 125 years of its existence. The congregation generally assumed that Americanization has been a good process and produced a progressive spirit in the congregation. As a result, many of the challenges posed during the years of its existence have been met and appropriate changes in the style and methods of ministry have been made. Understanding how the Americanization process has been good and right in Third Church calls for a closer look at the word and its implications.

"Americanization" is a difficult word to define exactly. Webster's dictionary gives this meaning: to Americanize is to make or become American in character, manners, methods, ideals, etc.[52] It is to assimilate American customs, speech, etc. This definition has often been referred to as the "melting pot" idea. The Rev. Dr. Henry E. Dosker, pastor of Third Church at the end of the nineteenth century [1889-94], affirmed Americanization as the melting pot idea when he said at the fiftieth anniversary celebration of the congregation in 1917: "Our Fathers [and Mothers] were in the Melting Pot.... These [people] understood that we came to America to be cast into the 'Melting Pot' and to be converted into *bona fide* Americans."[53] Therefore, he was a strong proponent for conducting worship at Third Church in English and paved the way for dropping the Dutch language completely. The melting pot idea has been criticized in recent years, however. Michael Novak, in his book, *The Rise of the Unmeltable Ethnics*, maintained that many Americans such as African Americans and Native Americans, were "unmeltable" because the cultural climate in America generally did not accept them into the American "Melting Pot." [54] Thus the current emphasis on "cultural pluralism" no longer considers it desirable that everyone in America speak only the English language or be blended into a homogeneity which disregards the distinctiveness of the great variety of ethnic cultures now existent in America.

For Third Church, Americanization has basically meant assimilation. Although many members of Third are descended from Dutch immigrants, there has been a considerable adaptation to prevailing American life styles and attitudes. But the description of Willis Jones, who as his name reveals was anything but Dutch, indicates that some attitudes and practices are not completely American. Third's love for solid, biblical preaching, its concern for maintaining a faithfulness to Reformational creedal formulations, its appreciation for traditional pastoral care, and similar traditions show resistance to total Americanization or assimiliation to mainline American Protestantism. Americanization became a threat to the distinctive Reformed heritage of the congregation, and it continues to influence the congregation to depart from its heritage and to blend more fully into the mainline Protestant scene.

The Americanization process, with the progressive attitude it engendered, seems to have had an unintended by-product of shifting Third Church into another social class. Originally Third's members, first-generation immigrants, were from lower classes, that is, people of a peasant background generally. In succeeding generations, its membership became broadly middle class and then lower upper class, where it now remains.[55] When Third was founded in 1867 through a peaceful division from its sister congregation, then the First Reformed Church and now the Pillar Christian Reformed Church, the congregation could be described as lower middle to middle middle-class. Many members were from the old peasant stock of the Netherlands who had come with Van Raalte to seek better economic and religious conditions in a new land. Isaac Cappon, one of the founders of Third Church and a member of the first consistory, was atypical in that he was a very successful businessman when Third Church was organized and very influential in the development of early Holland through all his business and financial enterprises. The beautiful home he built after the fire of 1871 was equal in cost to the newly rebuilt Third Reformed Church sanctuary. Unlike him, most early Third Church members were blue collar workers of modest means, such as farmers and factory workers. Cappon was soon joined by others who were attracted to Third Church and who became shapers of the economy, ethos, and culture of Holland, Michigan. Although Hope Reformed Church first attracted the prominent business and professional people because it was English speaking from the start, Third Church also began to attract such people by the turn of the century. College and seminary professors were added to the ranks by that time.[56] The pastors, Dosker, Dubbink, and Blekkink, masters of the pulpit, all made Third Church appealing to the intellectual and upwardly mobile members of the Holland community. When these three men became seminary professors they continued as members of the congregation. It was understood very early that Third Church ministers, beginning with Jacob Vander Meulen, son of the founder of Zeeland, Michigan, were to be good preachers with strong biblical emphases and be the best the denomination had to offer.

With quality preaching, good music, and the increasing personal financial resources of members, Third Church moved to an upper middle-class status after World War II. The Rev. Dr. Richard C. Oudersluys, professor of New Testament at Western Seminary, has noted that when his family joined Third in the early forties, many blue collar workers were still members of the congregation, but there were almost none by the 1990s.[57] The membership of Third now consists primarily of people who have income, cultural interests, positions, and education of the upper classes. Therefore, the present mission statement of Third Church can say that "high artistic standards" are expected in the church music. By no means are all members of the congregation from the upper classes, but Third Church does reflect an upper-class culture and ethos.

There are several key issues which confront the congregation of the Third Reformed Church in the final decade of the 20th century and at the beginning of the 21st, but the major challenge is in the realm of the spirit. The addition of new facilities, employing a staff which serves the congregation well, and continuing the tradition of effective lay leadership the congregation has made great strides forward. At the same time, it is challenged to believe that God planted this church for the purpose of ministering effectively to the neighborhood in which it has been located since its organization in 1867, as well as to the entire Holland area. Through the Reformed Church in America and other agencies, it continues to be called to serve throughout the nation and the world. Third's essential task is "to do battle for the Lord," to use old biblical imagery. Pastor Stam's sermon, "Is There Any Fight Left in Us?," which he preached August 21, 1994, focused on the centrality of the gospel to the life and work of the congregation and on being empowered by the Holy Spirit to accomplish the congregation's goals. This issue goes beyond the Americanization issue, beyond building programs and paying for new facilities, and beyond several issues which impinge on the church's ministry. As the church is willing to put on the "whole armor of God," it is prepared to carry out the mission which the Lord of the Church intends Third to have for the coming decades. Its longtime motto is still at the heart of its ministry: "To know Christ and to make Christ known."[58]

Appendices

Appendix 1

Members of Third Reformed Church in Church Vocations, 1867-1967

Third Church has sent many members into church vocations, mainly but not exclusively as ministers and spouses of ministers.* The list is comprehensive and inclusive. Many young men who went into the ministry during the first century of Third's existence came from other parts of the country but joined Third Church while they were students at Hope College or Western Theological Seminary. The congregation often gave them financial assistance or recommended them for financial assistance to the Board of Education of the Reformed Church in America. It is also very likely that some of them received financial assistance from the Classical Board of Benevolence Fund, which was started after the Great Holland Fire in 1872. Pastor Utterwick was instrumental in organizing that fund. Some of the people whose names are on the list were members in the Sunday school only.

Ainslie, Annetta L. McGilvra (Kenneth)
Althuis, Louise Cotts (Jacob J.)
Bast, the Rev. Dr. Henry
Blekkink, Agnes Stapelkamp (Victor J.)

* Entries for clergy spouses include the clergy member's name in parentheses following the entry.

Blekkink, the Rev. Dr. Victor J.
Boot, A. Ethel
Bos, the Rev. David
Braam, Harriet E. Steketee (Leonard M.)
Broek, the Rev. Dr. John Y.
Brouwer, Cornelia Prakken (Jacob)
Brunsting, the Rev. Luke A.
Cappon, Elizabeth
Colenbrander, Fannie Kooiker (Henry)
Coons, Lois Knooihuizen (William H.)
De Boer, the Rev. John L.
De Bruyn, Magdalena C. Cappon (Peter)
De Jong, the Rev. Jacob A.
De Pree, the Rev. J. James
De Velder, Harriet Boot (Walter)
De Weerd, Fred
De Young, Martha Van Dyke (Benjamin)
Dosker, the Rev. Richard
Dubbink, the Rev. Dr. Gerrit H.
Dubbink, Margaret Kollen (Gerrit H.)
Dykstra, the Rev. Broer D.
Dykstra, the Rev. Ellsworth C.
Dykstra, Irene Stapelkamp (John A.)
Esther, the Rev. Joseph R.
Esther, Marion Boot (Joseph R.)
Flikkema, Gertrude Sprietsma (Bernard M.)
Flikkema, Minnie Sprietsma (Bernard M.)
Flipse, the Rev. Dr. M. Eugene
Frego, Fr. Max
Gosselink, Henrietta Plasman (Marion G.)
Gruys, the Rev. William S.
Halko, Alma Stegenga (Andrew)
Harmeling, Jennie Verbeek (Henry)
Hazenberg, Lammetje Visscher (W.)
Hoekje, Hannah
Hogenboom, the Rev. Kermit
Holkeboer, Helen Van Dyke (Gilbert)
Ihrman, the Rev. Dr. Francis P.
Jacobs, Cora Vermeulen (Henry C.)
Jelsma, Eunice Scholten (Oscar)
Kammeraad, the Rev. Harold L.
Kastein, Ruth Kerkhof (Benjamin)
Kempers, Mabel Van Dyke (John R.)
Kleis, Carl M.
Koopman, the Rev. August J.
Kruidenier, Mrs. J.
Kruithof, the Rev. Frederick R.
Kuiken, the Rev. Peter
Louwenaar, Marguerite Oudemool (David)
Lubbers, the Rev. Egbert
Maat, the Rev. William G.
Marcus, Dr. Beth E.
Marcus, the Rev. Maurice
Martin, the Rev. James Dean
Maxam, Janet K.
McLean, Edith Cappon (Edwin P.)

Meengs, Gertrude Holleman (Chester)
Moerdyk, Cornelia Leenhouts (William J.)
Moerdyk, Dr. William J.
Muilenberg, Kate Slooter (Teunis W.)
Muller, Hermina Heil (John H.)
Muller, the Rev. John H.
Naberhuis, Herman
Neevel, Cornelia Nettinga (Alvin J.)
Nettinga, the Rev. Dr. James Z.
Nettinga, Katrina Zwemer (Siebe)
Nieuwsma, Jeanne Potter (John)
Olert, the Rev. John
Oltmans, the Rev. Dr. Theodore V.
Oltmans, Dr. W. Janet
Oosterhof, Johanna Van Ark (Albert)
Oudemool, the Rev. Arthur E.
Pasma, Olive Barnaby (Henry K.)
Pelgrim, the Rev. J. Carlton
Pickens, Elizabeth Zwemer (Claude L.)
Prakken, Esther
Reeverts, Emma
Rock, the Rev. Dr. Stanley
Rodstrom, Henrietta Oudemool (Charles)
Roskamp, the Rev. Bertrand A.
Ruigh, Jennie De Vries (David C.)
Smith, Beatrice Boot (Richard C.)
Stegeman, Gertrude Hoekje (Henry V.E.)
Stegenga, Margaret Beekman (Andrew)
Steketee, Jennie
Strickland, the Rev. Fenton
Sywassink, Mrs. George
Ter Borg, Amelia Sywassink (John)
Tritenbach, Marion Klaasen (Theodore G.)
Van Ark, Alice
Vander Hart, Marian Van Zyl (Norman E.)
Vander Hart, the Rev. Norman E.
Vandermel, Henrietta Kronemeyer (Cornelius)
Vander Meulen, the Rev. Jacob
Vanderschoor, Wilhelmina C. Riksen (Cornelius)
Vander Woude, Grace Frericks (Berend T.)
Vander Woude, the Rev. M. Paul
Van Dyke, Anna
Van Dyke, H. Milton
Van Eck, Dr. Edward
Van Eck, Mrs. Edward
Van Eck, Gwendolyn Kooiker (Paul K.)
Van Egmond, the Rev. Howard E.
Van Ess, Minnie De Bruyn (Jacob)
Van Heuvelen, Carrie De Feyter (Bernard)
Van Kalken, Dorothy Van Otterloo (Preston)
Van Lare, Deane Pelgrim (Elmer)
Van Putten, the Rev. Dr. J. Dyke
Van Raalte, the Rev. Nelson P.
Van Westenburg, Reka Kamferbeek (Isaac)

Van Zanten, Anna Vander Veen (Jacob J.)
Van Zomeren, Bertha Dalman (John)
Veenschoten, the Rev. Henry M.
Veldman, Adelaide Borgman (Jerry A.)
Veltman, John F.
Veneklasen, the Rev. James
Visscher, Gertrude Pieters (Maurice)
Voorhorst, Jennie
Waanders, Janet Wichers (David)
Warnshuis, Anna De Vries (A. Livingston)
Watermulder, Fannie Ver Beek (Gustavus A.)
Welmers, Dr. William E.
Westhof, Patricia De Boer (John C.)
Wezeman, Frieda Grote (Leonard)
Williams, Louise
Winter, the Rev. Jerry E.
Winter, the Rev. Jerry P.
Worthington, Henrietta Zwemer (William A.)
Wubbena, Lillian Martina Johanna De Feyter (Albert)
Yin, the Rev. Stanley
Zwemer, Evelyn
Zwemer, Marie K.
Zwemer, the Rev. Dr. Raymond
Zwemer, the Rev. Theodore

Appendix 2

Members of Third Church in Church Vocations, 1967-1995

The following list follows the guidelines found in Appendix 1.

Blaske, the Rev. Kathy Jo
Bos, the Rev. Linda June*
Camp, Lorrie Sherwood
Craig, the Rev. Stanley
Czirr, the Rev. Carl*
DenUyl, the Rev. Richard
Foster, the Rev. James N.
Gargano, Jeffrey
Gargano, Moira Poppen (Jeffrey)
Gowman, Jeffrey
Gowman, Kristen De Witt (Jeffrey)
Granberg-Michaelson, Karin (Wesley)
Granberg-Michaelson, the Rev. Wesley*
Holbrook, the Rev. Taylor
Jansen, Miho (Wayne)

*ordained in Third Church

Jansen, the Rev. Wayne
Kroondyk, the Rev. Henry M.
McCarty, the Rev. Ruth*
Monnett, Karin Marsilje
Munroe, Gretchen Yates (Jeffrey L.)
Munroe, the Rev. Jeffrey L.
Nieuwsma, the Rev. Mark E.*
Nieuwsma, Paula Nash (Mark E.)
Norden, Jean Boven (Stephen)
Nordstrom, Patricia Helder
Petersen, Deborah Moermond (F. Scott)
Petersen, the Rev. F. Scott
Phillips, the Rev. Nancy Van Wyk
Plasman, the Rev. Daniel*
Plasman, Mary Bruins (Daniel)
Schoep, the Rev. Arvin
Schoep, Nancy Slagter (Arvin)
Sharpe, the Rev. John, Jr.
Smith, the Rev. Vernon
Smith, Linda (Vernon)
Stolk, the Rev. Douglas*
Stolk, Mrs. Douglas
Twomey, the Rev. Burt C.
Twomey, Rose Mascorro (Burt)
Van Dyke, Nancy De Pree
Veldheer, the Rev. Kristine J.
Westphal, the Rev. Carol Petersen*
Westphal, Dr. Merold (Carol)
Zomermaand, the Rev. Conley A.*

Appendix 3

Elders of the Third Reformed Church

The lists in sections A and B are incomplete because the consistory minutes from 1896 to 1906 have been lost. These two lists were compiled through the untiring efforts of Myra Manting Weaver for the first edition of Third Church's history. List C has been obtained from church records since 1970.

A. The early period, 1867 to 1895:

Cappon, Isaac, 1876-1895
De Bruyn, Robbertus M., 1867-1869
Gunst, Peter, 1880-1895
Kerkhof, Jan, 1867-1876
Kieft, Fred, 1869-1883
Labots, Jacob, 1867-1877
Manting, Henry, 1873-1879
Ossenwaarde, Cornelius, 1884-1888
Schaddelee, Kommer, 1878-1880
Schols, Cornelis H., 1879-1895

Ver Beek, William, 1879
Van Zee, Eppink, 1867-1870
Vander Veen, Engbertus, 1890-1895

B. The period from 1907 to 1970:

Arendshorst, Bernard, 1966-1968
Beeuwkes, Fred, 1934-1937, 1940-1943, 1946-1949
Bennett, James, 1949-1952, 1958-1960
Bloemendaal, John, 1914-1921
Bolhuis, Frank, 1929-1932, 1938-1939
Bonnette, Gleon, 1957-1959, 1962-1964, 1967-1969
Bosman, Ivan, 1968-1970
Boven, Stanley, 1959-1961, 1964-1966
Brewer, Gordon, 1958-1960, 1963-1965, 1968-1970
Brink, Irwin, 1960-1962, 1965-1967
Cotts, Edward, 1933-1936
Dalman, Benjamin, 1948-1951, 1955-1957
De Boer, Charles, 1940-1943
Dekoning, Jay, 1948-1951, 1954-1956, 1959-1961
DuMez, Benjamin, 1916-1923, 1925-1928, 1933-1936, 1939-1942, 1945-1948
DuMez, John, 1910-1916, 1924-1927
Fleischer, Frank, 1958-1960, 1963-1965
Frissel, Harry, 1955-1957, 1960-1962, 1965-1967
Geerlings, Jacob, 1918-1923, 1925-1928, 1931-1934
Gunst, Peter, 1907-1911, 1917-1920
Hoffman, Judson, 1947-1948, 1951-1954, 1955-1958, 1961
Hoffman, Henry, 1930-1934
Huyser, John P., 1909-1916
Ihrman, Donald, 1967-1969
Jekel, Eugene, 1966-1968
Kammeraad, John, 1958-1960
Klaasen, Clarence, 1960-1962
Klaasen, Gerrit, 1929-1932, 1938-1941
Kleis, Clarence, 1937-1940, 1943-1946, 1949-1952, 1954-1956, 1959-1961, 1964-1966
Kooiker, John, 1929-1932, 1935-1938, 1941-1944
Kuiper, Chester, 1954-1956
Kuiper, Theodore, 1924-1925, 1929-1932, 1936-1939
Lampen, Albert, 1923-1926, 1928-1931, 1934-1937, 1940-1943, 1946-1949, 1952-1955, 1957-1960
Leenhouts, Jack, 1954-1956, 1959-1961, 1964-1966
Lindgren, Edgar, 1964-1966
Luidens, Preston, 1962-1963, 1966-1968
Meyer, Albert H., 1914-1923, 1926-1928
Miller, Carl, 1959-1960, 1963-1965
Moerdyk, William, 1950-1953, 1955-1957, 1961-1963
Mooi, George, 1937-1940

Muller, John, 1945-1946, 1949-1952, 1954-1956, 1959-1961, 1964-1966
Naberhuis, Bert, 1930-1934, 1937-1939, 1941-1944
Notier, Peter, 1921-1924, 1926-1929, 1932-1935, 1938-1941, 1944-1947, 1950-1951
Notier, Robert, 1953-1954, 1956-1958, 1961-1963, 1966-1968
Oosterhof, Willis, 1953-1954
Oosting, Dick, 1944-1947
Oosting, Harold, 1956-1958
Paul, Daniel, 1963-1965
Pelgrim, Henry, 1927-1930
Pessink, John, 1910-1913
Plasman, Benjamin, 1956-1958, 1962-1964, 1967-1969
Prins, James, 1968-1970
Rietberg, Roger, 1965-1967
Riksen, Bert, 1907-1908
Rinkus, Lambertus, 1947-1948
Schutmaat, George, 1950-1953, 1955-1957, 1962
Stephens, George, 1953-1955, 1957-1959, 1962-1964, 1967-1969
Tanis, Robert, 1954-1955
Ten Pas, Henry, 1960-1962, 1965-1967
Van Alsburg, John D., 1944-1945
Van Ark, Henry, 1912-1913, 1929-1931, 1933-1934, 1937-1940
Van Dahm, Thomas, Sr., 1946-1949, 1952
Van Dyke, Matthew, 1907-1920, 1924-1927, 1930-1932
Van Dyke, William E., 1914-1915, 1925-1929, 1933-1936, 1939-1942
Van Eerden, John, 1955-1957, 1960-1962, 1965-1967
Van Faasen, Albert, 1934, 1936-1937, 1942-1945, 1949-1952
Van Lente, Albert, 1961-1963
Van Lente, Dale, 1963-1965
Vande Bunte, Dick H., 1943-1946
Vander Borgh, Garrett, 1937-1938, 1941-1944, 1947-1950, 1953-1954, 1956-1958, 1961-1963, 1966-1968
Vander Hart, William E., 1926-1928, 1933-1936
Vander Veen, Engbertus, 1907-1913
Vander Ven, William, 1917-1922
Veldman, George J., 1922-1924
VerBeek, John, 1952-1955, 1957-1959, 1962-1964, 1967-1969
Ver Meer, Arnold, 1957-1959, 1962-1964
Welscott, James, 1954-1955
Wichers, Willard, 1953-1954
Wichers, Wynand, 1921-1924, 1926-1929, 1933-1936, 1942-1944, 1945
Zuidema, Jacob, 1945-1948

C. Classes of Elder, 1970 through 1998:

1970: Ivan Bosman, Gordon Brewer, Carl Miller, James Prins, and Dale Van Lente

1971: Stanley Boven, Jack Leenhouts, Edgar Lindgren, Daniel Paul, and Elliot Tanis

1972: Irwin Brink, Harry Frissel, Roger Rietberg, Henry Ten Pas, and Nathan Van Lente

1973: Bernard Arendshorst, Preston Luidens, Robert Notier, John Van Eerden, and Steven Van Grouw

1974: Eugene Jekel, Blaine Mays, Peter Schakel, Cornelius Steketee, and John Ver Beek

1975: Gleon Bonnette, Gordon Brewer, Donald Ihrman, Carl Miller, and Dale Van Lente

1976: Stanley Boven, Jack Daniels, Jantina Holleman, Jack Leenhouts, and Daniel Paul

1977: Irwin Brink, Erma Bruggink, Roger Rietberg, Elliot Tanis, and Henry Ten Pas

1978: William Arendshorst, Harry Frissel, Lars Granberg, Morris Tubergen, Willard Wichers, and Gerben Duthler (completing Irwin Brink's term)

1979: Irwin Brink, Elaine Jekel, Robert Notier, Lee Ten Brink, and Steven Van Grouw

1980: Paul DeMaagd, Etta Hesselink, Blaine Mays, Cornelius Steketee, and Elaine Tanis

1981: Gordon Brewer, Carl Miller, A. LeRoy Rediger, Dale Van Lente, and Merold Westphal

1982: Carol Granberg, Donald Ihrman, Eugene Jekel, Howard Kooiker, and Donald Maatman

1983: Preston Luidens, Peter Schakel, Frank Smith, Edward Stielstra, and Elliot Tanis

1984: Gleon Bonnette, Gus Feenstra, Harry Frissel, Jantina Holleman, and Morris Tubergen

1985: Irwin Brink, Henry Brinks, Elaine Jekel, Robert Sterken, and Douglas Walvoord

1986: Marilyn Franken, Eleanor Palma, Edwin Ratering, Steven Van Grouw, and Gerald Van Wyngarden

1987: Henrietta Bonnette, Eugene Campbell, Lars Granberg, Dale Van Lente, Merold Westphal, and Karen Schakel (completing Eugene Campbell's term)

1988: Mary De Witt, John Heyns, Donald Ihrman, Eugene Jekel, and Elaine Tanis

1989: Esther De Pree, Harold Ritsema, Gordon Stegink, Sandra Stielstra, Donald Van Lare, and Gerald Cox (completing Donald Van Lare's term)

1990: Delores Bechtel, Donald Cronkite, Bruce Ter Beek, Betty Lou Voskuil, and Marie Walvoord

1991: Irwin Brink, Janet De Young, Peter Handy, Beth Marcus, Peter Schakel, Carol Granberg (completing Bruce Ter Beek's term), and Jane Armstrong (completing Irwin Brink's term)

1992: Elaine Jekel, Edwin Ratering, Robert Sterken, Edward Stielstra, and Douglas Walvoord

1993: Henrietta Bonnette, Irwin Brink, Elliot Tanis, Donald Van Lare, and Gerald Van Wyngarden

1994: Gerald Cox, Jane Dykstra, Marilyn Franken, Etta Hesselink, and Jeff Munroe

1995: Mark Hiskes, Gay Hunsberger, Harold Ritsema, Morris Tubergen, and Kay Walvoord

1996: Phyllis Bruggers, Dennis De Witt, Dennis Gebben, William Moreau, and Deborah Sterken

1997: Donald Cronkite, John Lunn, Elly Muiderman, Lucille Schroeder, and Harold Van Dyke

1998: Carol Cox, Max De Pree, Mary Toppen-Palma, William Unzicker, and Douglas Walvoord

[The Class of 1987 began its term July 1, 1984, instead of January 1, 1984. See the *Third Generation*, June, 1983, for the announcement. Installation of new consistory members at mid-year began in the summer of 1984.]

Appendix 4

Deacons of the Third Reformed Church

A. The early period, 1867 to 1895.

Baert, A., 1880-83
Cappon, Isaac, 1867-74
De Jong, Cornelis, 1867-74
Diekema, Wiepke, 1889-95
Kieft, Frederick, 1867-69
Lukasse, J., 1871-73
Pessink, John, 1886-95
Schols, Cornelis H., 1875-79
Sprietsma, Simon, 1877-83
Te Roller, Derk, 1867-78
Van Ark, Herman, 1882-1907
Van Der Haar, Hein, 1879-88
Van Dyke, Teunis, 1872-95
Vander Veen, Engbertus, 1871-88
Visscher, Arend, 1889-92
Werkman, E., 1874-78
Winter, Peter, 1893-95

B. The period from 1907-1970.

Arendshorst, Bernard, 1939-42, 1947-50, 1953-54, 1961-63
Arendshorst, William, Sr., 1929-32, 1937-39
Arendshorst, William, Jr., 1959-61, 1965-67
Barkema, Robert, 1959-61, 1964-66
Beeuwkes, Fred, 1920-24, 1926-29
Bolhuis, Jack, 1963-65, 1968-70
Bonnette, Gleon, 1952-55
Bos, Alvin, 1955, 1957-59
Bos, Thomas, 1966-68
Bosman, Ivan, 1933-35
Bosman, Nelson, 1941-44, 1947-50
Boundy, Bruce 1967-1969
Boven, Ronald, 1962-64, 1967-69
Boven, Stanley, 1948-51, 1954-56
Brower, Paul, 1941-42
Buter, Harvey, 1954-56, 1959-61, 1964-66
Cook, Alvin, 1949-52, 1954-56, 1960-62
Cook, Carl, 1948-51, 1954-56, 1959-61, 1965-67
Dalman, Andrew, 1962-64, 1968-70
Dalman, Benjamin, 1933-34, 1936-37, 1940-44
Dekker, Bert, 1934-37
De Fouw, Clarence, 1952-55, 1957-59, 1963-65
De Goede, John, 1918-23
De Haan, Alwin, 1966-68
De Koning, Jay, 1930-34, 1936-40, 1942-45
De Kraker, John, 1945-48, 1951-54, 1956-58, 1961-63
De Pree, Bernard, 1943-46
De Vries, Milo, 1926-28, 1937-39
Diekema, Wilson, 1944-47
DuMez, Benjamin, 1910-15

DuMez, John, 1907-09
DuMez, Theodore, 1934-37, 1943-44
Eby, William C., 1926-29
Feenstra, Gus, 1963-65, 1968-70
Frego, Donald, 1968-70
Geerlings, Henry, 1911-14
Groenewoud, Gordon, 1957
Hamm, Robert, 1958-60
Heneveld, Lowell, 1964-66
Hoffman, Judson, 1938-41, 1945-46
Huyser, John P., 1907-08
Jalving, Marvin, 1958-60, 1963-65, 1968
Kardux, Lane, 1930-32
Karsten, Nelson, 1955-57
Ketel, Henry, 1921-29, 1933
Klaasen, Russell, 1953-54, 1956-58, 1961-63, 1966-68
Klaasen, Clarence, 1955-57
Knooihuizen, Ray, 1942-45, 1948-51
Kooiker, Howard, 1952-55, 1957-59, 1962-64
Kooiker, John, 1910-14, 1917-26, 1928
Kooiker, Kenneth, 1960-62
Kuiper, Chester, 1949-52
Kuiper, Theodore, 1921-23, 1928
Landaal, Hendrik, 1907-08
Lievense, Donald, 1965-67
Lievense, Jacob, 1930-34, 1937-40
Lokker, Chris J., 1909-14, 1916-19
Luidens, Preston, 1957-59
Maatman, Donald, 1960-62, 1965-67
Marcus, Jack, 1929-32, 1935-39, 1942-44
Muller, John, 1930-34, 1937-40, 1943-44
Naberhuis, Bert, 1929
Notier, Peter, 1914-20
Notier, Robert, 1947-50
Oosting, Harold, 1950-53
Oudemool, Martin, 1926-28, 1931-34
Paarlberg, John, 1967-69
Paul, Daniel, 1958-60
Pessink, John, 1907-09
Prakken, Nicholas, 1907-09
Rediger, LeRoy, 1960-62, 1965-67, 1970
Riksen, Russell, 1956-58, 1962-64
Rinkus, Lambertus, 1944-46
Schipper, John H., 1929-32
Slenk, Elvin, 1964-66
Soderberg, Ray, 1943-46
Steketee, Henry, 1928-31, 1934-37
Tazelaar, Arthur, 1962-64, 1967-69
Todd, Carl, 1961-63, 1966-68
Van Ark, Henry, 1907-11
Van Ark, Peter, 1924-27
Van Beveren, Leslie, 1967-69
Van Dahm, Thomas, Sr., 1940-44
Van Dahm, Thomas, Jr., 1957-59
Vande Bunte, Lewis, 1958-60, 1963-65, 1969-70
Vander Borgh, Garrett, 1929-32, 1935
Vander Hart, William E., 1915-22
Van der Riet, George, 1923-26
Van Dyk, Albert B., 1933-36, 1939-42

Van Dyke, Cornelius, 1921-25, 1927-28, 1932-25, 1938-40
Van Dyke, William E., 1909-13
Van Eck, Edward, 1955-57
Van Eerden, John, 1944-47, 1950-53
Van Faasen, Albert, 1925-27
Van Lente, Albert, 1938-41, 1945-48, 1951-54, 1956-58
Van Lente, Dale, 1958-60
Van Lente, Nathan, 1964-66
Van Osterhout, Theodore, 1955-57
Van Spyker, Edward, 1960-62
Van Tatenhove, Melvin, 1959-61
Verburg, Simon, 1915-19,
Vollink, Andrew, 1951-54, 1957-58, 1961-63, 1966-68
Vredenberg, [first name unknown], 1918-19
Weaver, Duncan, 1946-49
Welscott, James, 1938-41
Westveer, William J., 1912-17
Wichers, Willard C., 1946-49
Wichers, Wynand, 1920
Wiersma, Benjamin, 1924-27
Zuidema, Jacob, 1921-25, 1927-31, 1933-36, 1939-42

C. Classes of Deacons, 1970 to 1998.

1970: Jack Bolhuis, Andrew Dalman, Gus Feenstra, Don Frego, and Marvin Jalving

1971: Robert Barkema, Harvey Buter, Robert Kuiper, Robert Riemersma, and Elvin Slenk

1972: William Arendshorst, Ronald Boeve, Donald Lievense, LeRoy Rediger, and Lewis Vande Bunte

1973: Paul DeMaagd, Donald Den Uyl, Kenneth Koning, Donald Maatman, and Lee Ten Brink

1974: Thomas Bos, Ronald Boven, Dennis DeWitt, Erwin Ter Haar, and Wayne Westenbroek

1975: David Barber, Jack Bolhuis, Morris Peterson, Glenn Riksen, and Arthur Tazelaar

1976: Robert Barkema, Harvey Buter, Bruce Formsma, Dennis Gebben, and Robert Kuiper

1977: Ronald Boeve, Gus Feenstra, Thomas Piaget, Elvin Slenk, and Bruce Ter Beek

1978: Tom Bolhuis, Phyllis De Haan, John Hutchinson, Ronald Knutson, and Daniel Miller

1979: Robert Benningfield, Donald Den Uyl, Randall Driesenga, Dale Dykema, and Robert Klein

1980: Jon Bechtel, Thomas Bos, Mark de Roo, Carol Gargano, and Wayne Westenbroek

1981: Jack Bolhuis, Joel Bouwens, Steven De Young, Andrew Mulder, and Morris Peterson

1982: Robert Barkema, Harvey Buter, Bruce Formsma, Robert Kuiper, and James Vander Meer

1983: Ronald Boeve, Sue Hutchinson, William Moreau, Elvin Slenk, and Bruce Ter Beek

1984: Delores Bechtel, Kevin Neckers, Thomas Piaget, Richard Vande Bunte, and Richard Vandervelde

1985: Robert Benningfield, Phyllis De Haan, Donald Den Uyl, Dale Dykema, and William Lawton

1986: Kathryn Bates, Kris De Pree, Mark de Roo, Carol Gargano, and John Hutchinson

1987: Jon Bechtel, Joel Bouwens, Steven De Young, Edward Marsilje, and Andrew Mulder

1988: Everett Albers, Harvey Buter, Bruce Formsma, Morris Peterson, and James Vander Meer

1989: Ronald Boeve, Mark Bonnette, Robert Carlson, David Carothers, and William Ten Pas

1990: Trudy Berkel, Richard De Witt, Dennis Gebben, William Moreau, and D. Leroy Stageman

1991: Kevin Clark, Dale Dykema, Susan Formsma, William Lawton, and Richard Smith

1992: Kris De Pree, John Hoekstra, Sue Hutchinson, William Segrist, and Ella Weymon

1993: Greg Caskey, Steven De Young, Edward Marsilje, Karl Meyer, and James Voogd

1994: Thomas Bos, Joel Bouwens, Mary DeJonge-Benishek, Jody Handy, and Mike Rannow

1995: Ronald Boeve, Mark Bonnette, David Carothers, Andrew Mulder, and Douglas Willis

1996: John Arendshorst, David Armstrong, David Bast, Christopher Cook, and Nancy Heyns

1997: Tim Du Mez, Susan Formsma, John Hutchinson, Lydia Knowles, and Willis Weymon

1998: James Campbell, Douglas Finn, Cindy Hiskes, Timothy Hoffman, and Mary Ann Knowles

Appendix 5

Superintendents of the Sunday School

Isaac Cappon, 1868-1890
Arend Visscher, 1890-19?
Henry Pelgrim, 19?-1919
William J. Westveer, 1920-1926
Wynand Wichers, 1927-1928
Fred Beeuwkes, 1929-1932
Garrett Vander Borgh, 1938-1944
Clarence Kleis, 1945-1949
Benjamin Plasman, 1950-1954
Jack Leenhouts, 1955-1959
Harry Frissel, 1959-1962
Dale Van Lente, 1963-1965
Daniel Paul, 1966-1968
Eugene Jekel, 1969-1970
Lee Ten Brink, 1970-1972
Bruce TerBeek, 1972-1975
Elaine Tanis, 1975-1978
Thomas Piaget, 1978-1980
Pat Jones, 1980-1984
Nancy Gebben, 1984-1987
Mark Verhulst, 1987-1989
Thomas Piaget, 1989-1992
Everett Albers, 1992-

Appendix 6

Presidents of the Ladies' Aid

Margaret Kollen Dubbink, 1898-1905
Henrietta E. Meerdink Blekkink, 1906-1913
Mrs. Martin Flipse, 1914-1919
Mrs. Sam Habing, 1920-1922
Christina Leeusenkamp Van Dyke, 1923-1926
Margaret Beekman Stegenga, 1927
Margaret Beekman Stegenga Van Faasen, 1928
Alida De Pree Wichers, 1929-1930

Theresa Van Vulpen Notier, 1930
Jennie Van Alsburg Ihrman, 1931-1932
Mrs. Eli Arnold, 1933-1934
Susanne Dragt Vander Borgh, 1935-1936
Mrs. George Van der Riet, 1937-1938
Sena Kooiker Du Mez, 1939
Lois Dressel Bosman, 1940-1941
Nell DeValois Van't Hof, 1942-1943
Lois Thoms Kuiper, 1944-1945
Mrs. Wilson Diekema, 1946-1947
Gertrude Sprietsma Flikkema, 1948-1949
Susanne Dragt Vander Borgh, 1950
Elsie Jalving, 1951-1952
Fannie Plasman Van Dyk, 1953
Nell Van Haitsma Wichers, 1954
Thelma DeFeyter Drake, 1955

Appendix 7

Presidents of the Women's Missionary Society

Hannah Te Roller, 1896-1897
Martha Diekema Kollen, 1897-1899
Magdalena Cappon DeBruyn, 1900-1904
Margaret Kollen Dubbink, 1905-1911
Magdalena Cappon DeBruyn, 1912-1915
Henrietta E. Meerdink Blekkink, 1916-1922
Katrina M. Zwemer Nettinga, 1923-1929
Mrs. Thomas E. Welmers, 1930-1937
Margaret Kollen Dubbink, 1938-1940
Alida De Pree Wichers, 1941-1943
Mrs. John Wesselink, 1944-1946
Margaret Kollen Dubbink, 1947
Mrs. John Wesselink, 1948
Mrs. John Vander Meulen, 1949-1950
Kate Everhard DePree, 1951-1953
Bertha Dalman Van Zomeren, 1954-1955

Appendix 8

Presidents of the Women's Missionary Auxiliary

Theresa Van Vulpen Notier, 1925-1926
Martha Schoon Pelgrim, 1927-1928
Mrs. John H. Schipper, 1929-1930
Mrs. John Vander Meulen, 1931-193?
Margaret Beekman Stegenga Van Faasen, 1938
Henrietta Warnshuis, 1939-1941
Susanne Dragt Vander Borgh, 1942-1943
Clara Reeverts, 1944-1945
Martha Schoon Pelgrim, 1946
Marian De Young Oudersluys, 1947-1948
Margaret Van Raden, 1948
Fannie Plasman Van Dyk, 1949-1951
Maxine Kooiker Wilson, 1952-1953
Marilyn Shisler Kooiker, 1954-1955

Appendix 9

Presidents of Reformed Church Women's Ministries

Dorothy Stephens, 1956-1957
Marilyn Kooiker, 1958
Susanne Vander Borgh, 1959-1960
Elizabeth Koeppe, 1961
Bernice Dykstra, 1962-1963
Marie Van Eerden, 1964-1965
Lillian Dalman, 1966-1967
Lois Vande Bunte, 1968
Phyllis De Haan, 1969-1971
Evelyn Rietberg, 1971
Edna Ten Pas, 1972-73
Eleanor Cotts, 1973-1974
Lucille Hoeksema, 1974-1975
Winifred Kooiker, 1976-1978
Kay Duthler, 1978-1980
Henrietta Bonnette, 1980-1981
Mary Kansfield, 1982-1984

Margaret Pott, 1984-1985
Sandy Stielstra, 1985-1986
Esther Vande Bunte, 1986-1987
Beth Marcus, 1987-1988
Kathryn Bates, 1988-1989
Lynne Bonnette, 1989-1990
Delores Bechtel, 1990-1991
Carol Cox, 1991-1992
Barbara Lawton, 1992-1993
Diana Marsilje, 1993-1994
Esther Vande Bunte, 1994-

Appendix 10

Church Organists

Hannah Te Roller, 1889-January, 1908
Minnie Sprietsma, 1905-1912
Henrietta Warnshuis, 1912-1918
Jennie Karsten, 1918-1936
Kenneth R. Osborne, 1937-1940
James H. Mearns, 1940-1942
Anna Ruth Poppen, 1942
Mildred W. Schuppert, 1942-1950; Associate Organist, 1950-1988
Roger Rietberg, 1950-1995

Appendix 11

Church Choir Directors

Senior Choir:

Cornelis De Jong, 1874-?
John Vander Sluis, 1893-1923
Mrs. W. J. Fenton, 1924
Grace Mills, 1925
A. C. Van Raalte Gilmore, 1925-1926
Martha Barkema, 1927-1929
Nicholas Gosselink, 1930
Howard Schade, 1931
Hazel Paalman, 1931-1933
Jean Herman, 1933-1934
Trixie Moore, 1935-1937
Kenneth R. Osborne, 1937-1940
Robert Cavanaugh, 1940-1943
Trixie Moore, 1943-1947
Elaine Ackerson Soderberg, 1947-1949
Barbara Lampen, 1949-1950
Roger Rietberg, 1950-1995

Junior Choir:

Roger Rietberg, 1950-1963
Evelyn Huizenga Rietberg, 1963-1989
Lisa Roorda, 1989-1990
Nancy Neuman, 1990-1991
Marty Killinger Neifer, 1991-1995

Appendix 12

Members of Third Church Who Served on the Board of the Holland Public Schools

Isaac Cappon, 1874-1894
the Rev. Henry Utterwick, 1875
Engbertus Vander Veen, 1882-1894
Arend Visscher, 1884-1895
Gerrit J. Diekema, 1894-1897
Henry Geerlings, 1898-1944
Derk J. Te Roller, 1906-1907
Fred Beeuwkes, 1914-1944
Henry Pelgrim, 1916-1919
George Mooi, 1920-1930, 1931-1937
Wynand Wichers, 1925-1930
William Arendshorst, Sr., 1927-1936, 1937-1940
John Olert, 1933-1951
Albert Lampen, 1934-1953
Albert Van Lente, 1936-1948
Jay De Koning, 1944-1953
Clarence Klaasen, 1945-1948
Alvin J. Cook, 1952-1963
Bernard Arendshorst, 1955-1964
Harry Frissel, 1958-1965
Harvey J. Buter, 1961-1969
Mrs. Lowell Heneveld, 1965-1968
Ronald Boeve, 1981-1989
Reed Brown, c. 1982-1986
Kevin Clark, 1994-
Deborah P. Sterken, 1995-

Appendix 13

The Memorial Windows, 1946

THE ANNUNCIATION.
In memory of Henry Pelgrim, Sr. (1855-1944); Mrs. Henry Pelgrim, Sr. (1859-1946); and Henry G. Pelgrim, Jr. (1991-1919).

THE ANNUNCIATION TO THE SHEPHERDS.
In loving memory of John Vander Sluis (1860-1943).

THE NATIVITY.
In loving memory of Thaddeus W. Taft (1878-1937).

THE FLIGHT INTO EGYPT.
In memory of Gradus Van Ark, builder of this church; Aaltje (Oldenhof) Van Ark and Herman Van Ark; Reany (Winter) Van Ark, by Peter H. Van Ark, grandson and son, and Johanna (Boda-Kardux) Van Ark.

THE BOY CHRIST IN THE TEMPLE.
In memory of the young men of the church who died while serving in World War II. Presented by the Sunday school.

THE BAPTISM.
In loving memory of Herman Vaupell, Kate Louise Vaupell.

THE SERMON ON THE MOUNT.
In memory of the departed friends and members of the Senior Christian Endeavor Society by Senior C. E. Alumni.

GETHSEMENE.
In loving memory of John DuMez (1863-1928) by Mrs. John DuMez and children.

THE RESURRECTION.
In loving memory of Arend Bosman (1868-1939).

THE ASCENSION.
In honor of the men and women of Third Reformed Church who served their country in World War II by the Ladies Aid Society.

Appendix 14

The Ordained and Installed Ministers of the Third Reformed Church and the Years of their Ministry

Jacob Vander Meulen, 1868-1871
Henry Utterwick, 1872-1880
Dirk Broek, 1880-1888
Henry E. Dosker, 1889-1895
Gerrit H. Dubbink, 1895-1904
Evert J. Blekkink, 1905-1913
Martin Flipse, 1913-1920
James M. Martin, 1921-1934
William Van't Hof, 1936-1945
Jacob J. Sessler, Senior Minister, 1946-1949
Harold De Roo, Associate Minister, 1948-1949
Christian H. Walvoord, Senior Minister, 1950-1958
Jerry A. Veldman, Associate Minister, 1955-1962
Russell Vande Bunte, Senior Minister, 1959-1969
Mark O. Walvoord, Associate Minister, 1967-1974
Robert J. Hoeksema, Senior Minister, 1971-1978
John D. Paarlberg, Minister of Education, 1976-1978; Minister of Parish Life, 1979-1981
Kathy Jo Blaske, Minister of Education, 1978-1988
Willis A. Jones, Senior Minister, 1979-1986
Harold M. Delhagen, Minister of Parish Life, 1982-1985
Ronald M. Franklyn, Associate Minister, 1986-1991
Ervin G. Roorda, Senior Minister, 1987-1990
Dennis N. Voskuil, Acting Senior Minister, 1990-1992
Steven S. Stam, Senior Minister, 1992-
Kathryn Davelaar, Associate Minister, 1993-

Appendix 15

Special Events for the Celebration of the One Hundred Twenty-Fifth Anniversary of Third Reformed Church, 1992 and 1993

September 25: The Anniversary Dinner at Evergreen Commons.

September 26: Tours of Third Church's historic sanctuary, historical exhibits, and tea in the Fellowship Hall, 2-4 p.m.

September 27: The Rev. Dr. Edwin G. Mulder, General Secretary of the Reformed Church in America, guest preacher at the morning services. The sermon title: "Affirm Your Past; Embrace Your Future." The Rev. Dr. Steven S. Stam, senior pastor, worship leader for the evening vesper service.

October 25: Organ concert by David Hurd, professor of church music and organist, General Theological Seminary, New York City.

November 1 to 19: A mini-course, "Understanding Third Reformed Church Through a Review of Its History," by Elton J. Bruins.

December 6 to 20: A mini-course, "Our Stained Glass Windows—The Gospel in Art" by Marie J. Walvoord.

December 13: A service of lessons and carols.

February 26-28: A weekend with the Rev. Dr. Lewis Smedes, professor of Christian ethics, Fuller Theological Seminary, Pasadena, California.

April 18: A hymn festival celebrating our Reformed heritage with Brian Wren, minister in the United Reformed Church, Great Britain.

April 25: Organ concert by Andrew Lumsden, organist and master of the choristers, Litchfield Cathedral, Great Britain.

June 13: A service of recommitment, with sermon, "Back to the Future," by Pastor Stam in Dimnent Memorial Chapel, followed by brunch at Evergreen Commons.

Appendix 16

Significant Events in the Life of the Third Reformed Church, 1967-1993

May 12, 1967: the newly restored sanctuary was dedicated. A new cornerstone was set in place the week before.

Sept. 9, 1967: on the exact date of the founding of Third Church, the congregation gathered in the Holland Civic Center for a centennial anniversary dinner. Willard C. Wichers chaired the centennial celebration.

Oct. 6, 1968: the time of the evening worship service was moved from 7 p.m. to 5 p.m. After experimentation with various starting times, the congregation eventually settled on 6 p.m. and other Holland Reformed churches followed suit.

Sept., 1969: the church again began to publish a monthly newsletter, but it was not until August, 1980, that it received the name, *The Third Generation*.

Sept., 1969: Ivan and Adlyn Bosman suggested the "Congregational Coffee" after morning worship. More than 250 people were present at the first one, and it has continued as a practice since that time.

Nov. 16, 1969: the congregation bade farewell to Russell and Lois Vande Bunte, who were moving to Ridgewood, New Jersey, to serve the First Reformed Church.

Dec. 3, 1969: the Women's Missionary Group of the Women's Guild disbanded.

Feb. 2, 1970: the consistory approved the installation of a branch of the Holland Day Care. Margaret Steffens and Nell Wichers headed the committee.

Apr. 1-4, 1970: several Third Church members attended the Festival of Evangelism in Detroit's Cobo Hall. Many koinonia groups were organized in the congregation as a result of that festival.

May 31, 1970: a historical marker was unveiled by Lavina Cappon, whose father, Isaac, was instrumental in having Third Church rebuilt following the Great Fire of 1871 when Third's three-year old sanctuary was consumed.

Oct. 15, 1970: the Special Education Catechism classes began. Each student would have her/his own teacher.

Jan. 3, 1971: it was announced in the church bulletin that the Mission Memorial Fund would be established and presented for approval to the congregation at the January 19 congregational meeting.

Feb. 14, 1971: Robert Hoeksema was installed as senior pastor.

Mar. 28, 1971: the Discussion Class sponsored a panel of the candidates for mayor, Louis Hallacy II and L. W. Lamb, Jr., to ascertain their ideas concerning social issues facing the Holland community.

May, 1971: Willard Wichers announced that the sanctuary of Third Church was placed on the National Register of Historic Places.

Oct. 6-9, 1971: twelve members of the congregation attended the RCA Mission Festival in Milwaukee, Wisconsin.

Oct. 1, 1972: Pastor Mark Walvoord organized the weekday Youth Club.

Jan. 7, 1973: two mini-courses for adults were listed in the bulletin. This new program idea which many churches soon adopted, was inaugurated by Pastor Walvoord.

Mar. 23-25, 1973: the Family Affair Festival was celebrated.

Jan. 6, 1974: Jantina Holleman was ordained as the first woman elder at Third Church.

Nov. 17, 1974: Mark Walvoord concluded his pastorate at Third Church and assumed the pastorate at the Parkview Reformed Church in Cleveland, Ohio.

March, 1975: "Action Because We Care," or "ABC" as the program was called, was organized by Sylvia Tubergen, Linda Smith, and Jackie Van

Wieren. The current parish system developed out of this program.

Jan., 1976: "Our Song of Hope," a confessional statement written by a member of the congregation, the Rev. Dr. Eugene Heideman, was introduced to the congregation. Our own Minister of Music, Roger Rietberg, composed the music for it.

March 13-14, 1976: the Religious Arts Festival was held under the leadership of Etta Hesselink.

July 4, 1976: the nation's bicentennial was celebrated at a special morning worship service.

July 18, 1976: the Rev. John Paarlberg was installed as minister of education.

Aug. 13-17, 1976: eleven Third Church members attended the RCA Jubilee '76 at Slippery Rock, Pennsylvania.

Jan., 1977: Pastors Robert Hoeksema and John Paarlberg attended the Bethel Bible Series Seminar in Madison, Wisconsin. The program began at Third Church in February.

Summer, 1977: Cornelia Tillema announced that members of the Reformed Church Women of Third Church had baked 264 birthday cakes for Hope College students the previous year.

Apr. 9, 1978: the congregation celebrated the 350th anniversary of the Reformed Church in America, which had been founded on Manhattan Island in 1628.

May 21, 1978: the congregation voted to call Kathy Jo Blaske as director of Christian education. After she had been on staff for one year, she was ordained and installed as the first woman pastor of Third Church on October 28, 1979.

May 20, 1979: the Rev. Willis A. Jones preached his inaugural sermon entitled, "Lord of the Dance."

Oct. 6, 1979: the Simpler Life Styles workshop was conducted.

Nov. 11, 1979: the U. S. Air Force Academy Chorale sang several anthems at the morning service. The chorale included a member of Third Church, John Miller, son of Carl and Marjorie Miller.

Nov. 18, 1979: Pastor Jones instituted the "Mindings" program, which has continued as an annual event. Members of the church bring small gifts to the chancel in the morning service. After the service, the gifts are taken to sick, shut-ins, and persons who lost loved ones during the year.

Feb., 1980: it was announced in the *Third Generation* that Third, St. Francis, and First United Methodist Churches covenanted together for neighborhood involvement. The Interparish Council developed from this covenant.

May, 1980: Pastor Paarlberg announced that the Stephens Ministry program would be inaugurated in the fall.

March, 1981: the Lenten Parish Bible Studies program was inaugurated by Pastor Jones.

July 28, 1981: the Chang family arrived in Holland from Cambodia. The family was sponsored by the congregation.

Sept., 1981: with the completion of the renovation of the chapel, the pews were given to the Wah-Bun Chapel, Ponemah, Minnesota, an Indian gospel mission.

Sept. 13, 1981: double morning worship services were inaugurated.

Dec. 31, 1981: John Paarlberg concluded his ministry at Third to assume the pastorate at the Pitcher Hill Community Church, North Syracuse, New York.

Feb. 7, 1982: Ruth E. McCarty was ordained at Third Church. She served as an interim associate pastor between the pastorate of John Paarlberg and Harold Delhagen.

May 2, 1982: the congregation voted to call the Rev. Harold Delhagen as associate minister. He was installed July 11.

Sept. 19, 1982: the new organ, which was built by Robert Sipe of Dallas, Texas, was dedicated. Gerre Hancock, organist of St. Thomas Episcopal Church of New York City, played the dedicatory concert November 14.

Sept. 29, 1982: Kerk Night was inaugurated, following the discontinuance of evening worship services.

Apr. 16, 1983: 116 Third Churchers marched in the CROP Walk.

Sept., 1983: Kid's Club was inaugurated by the congregations of St. Francis, First United Methodist, and Third Church, congregations belonging to the Interparish Council. The club was open to the children of the neighborhood. It met at Third Church under the direction of Alice Vogel.

Oct., 1983: Chairperson John Hutchinson reported in the *Third Generation* that 176 men, women, and children of Third Church participated in the Annville project that year. The project cost $24,638.96. "Our work groups directly touched more than 80 lives through 50+ home improvement projects in five Kentucky counties. Our summer staff and volunteer Bible School teachers from Third reached approximately 700 children from pre-schoolers to high school seniors. We did not change Jackson County, but we did make a difference as attested to by the many letters of gratitude that we have received," Mr. Hutchinson reported.

March, 1984: consistory approved our support of the new church start in Dublin, Ohio. A daughter of Third Church, Jean Boven, and her husband, the Rev. Stephen Norden, were called to organize the new congregation.

July 29, 1984: Third Church purchased a van which was available for transportation to those in need of that service.

Dec., 1984: Third Church reached a peak in membership: 899 communicant members, and total souls in the congregation numbered 1,179. Ninety-one new members were received that year.

May 28, 1985: the "Third Reformed Church Women" celebrated the 25th anniversary of Reformed Church Women, a program which had its inspiration in the reorganization of women's work at Third Church under Marie Walvoord in the 1950s.

Sept. 8, 1985: the new RCA hymnbook, *Rejoice in the Lord*, was dedicated. The hymnbooks were given in memory of Clarence Klaasen by his family. Our minister of music, Roger Rietberg, and former member of the congregation, Norman Kansfield, were members of the hymnbook committee.

Dec. 31, 1985: Harold Delhagen concluded his ministry at Third Church to assume the pastorate at the First Reformed Church of Hudson, New York.

Mar. 2, 1986: the New Jersey project was launched under the leadership of Kris De Pree and Dr. Lars Granberg.

July 20, 1986: the congregation bade farewell to Willis and Pat Jones, who left to assume the pastorate of the Wyckoff Reformed Church of Wyckoff, New Jersey.

Aug. 21, 1986: the Rev. Ronald Franklyn arrived in Holland to begin his work as associate pastor.

July 7, 1987: the new senior pastor, the Rev. Ervin Roorda, began his ministry at Third Church.

May 31, 1988: Kathy Jo Blaske accepted a position on the staff of the Synod of Albany, RCA, and concluded her ministry at Third Church.

Sept., 1988: the Children and Worship program replaced the Junior Church program.

Nov., 1988: it was announced in the *Third Generation* that Dr. Donald Cronkite was the contact person for those persons interested in participating in the "Housing Opportunity Made Equitable" program.

July, 1989: Church Treasurer Harvey Buter announced that the congregation pledged $138,000 to the "Putting People in Mission" program of the RCA.

Sept. 12, 1989: the elders approved the admission of children to the Lord's Supper.

Jan. 1, 1989: Karen Schakel began her work as director of Christian education.

Aug. 1, 1990: the Rev. Dr. Dennis Voskuil assumed the position of acting senior pastor following the resignation of Pastor Roorda earlier in the year.

June 16, 1991: George Hunsberger and Janet De Young introduced the Master Planning program to the newly appointed committee.

June, 1992: Beth Marcus, an elder at Third Church, was elected the first woman president of the General Synod of the Reformed Church in America.

Aug. 23, 1992: the Rev. Dr. Steven S. Stam was installed as senior minister of the Third Reformed Church.

Nov. 8, 1992: a Japanese worship service was initiated at Third Church and has continued monthly.

May 23, 1993: the Rev. Kathryn Davelaar's letter of acceptance of the position of associate minister was read to the congregation by the vice president of Consistory, Gerald Cox, at morning worship. She was installed June 20, 1993.

June 13, 1993: a service of rededication and commitment was held in the Dimnent Memorial Chapel on the campus of Hope College. This service concluded the year-long celebration of the congregation's 125th anniversary of the founding of the congregation on September 9, 1867.

Appendix 17

Mission Statement of the Third Reformed Church

The mission of Third Reformed Church is to enable us, its members, to grow in our commitment to Jesus Christ, to motivate us through the Holy Spirit to become actively involved in Christian service, and to share with each other and those outside our fellowship the joy of the new life we have in Christ. Historically, this mission has been expressed in our motto: **"To know Him and to make Him known."** To fulfill our mission, with God's help, we will:

emphasize the Biblically grounded preaching of God's word within worship services which are liturgically in harmony with Reformed theology and high artistic standards;

expand our traditional support of missionary outreach to include increased emphasis on local evangelism and support of our members to become directly involved in Christian outreach;

build creatively on past excellence in Christian education stressing growth in knowledge of what it means to be a Christian in the world today for both children and adults of all ages;

grow in building a friendly, caring spirit towards each other and strangers;

continue our long-standing denominational loyalty tempered with a strong spirit of ecumenism.

Third Reformed Church has a distinguished tradition of being a progressive congregation and will continue to seek new ways to serve our Lord as the Holy Spirit guides and directs us.

Appendix 18

Hymn texts by Brian Wren,
Commissioned by Third Reformed Church.

"We Are the Music Angels Sing"

In Memory of Tommy Rietberg

We are the music angels sing:
short or long,
each life a song,
a treasured offering.

A child, brief skylark, soaring young,
fell from sight,
yet all that flight
by Gabriel is sung.

The melody, though short it seems,
deeper grows:
heavn's music flows,
developing its themes.

Discordant grief and aching night,
love transposed,
will be composed
in symphonies of light.

And every human pain and wrong
shall be healed
for Christ revealed
a new and better song.

We are the music angels sing:
short or long,
each life a song,
a treasured offering.

"Sing Praises Old and New"

Composed for the 125th Anniversary of Third Reformed Church

Sing praises old and new,
past and present join in one.
Old covenants renew:
new commitments have begun.
God's soaring purpose spans
all ages, lives and lands.
Christ's open, wounded hands
past and present join in one.
Word, from the heart of God,
costly, unexpected grace,
Love, making all things good,
Light of all the human race,
Hail, Wisdom, deep and vast,
shining in Israel's past,

raising the least and last:
costly, unexpected grace!

Great Spirit, make us wise,
doors of promise open wide.
Through evil's deadly lies
truth and goodness set aside,
faith never stands alone,
hope rolls away the stone,
love makes your presence known,
doors of promise open wide.

People of hope, be strong!
Love is making all things new.
Lift our united song,
show what faith can dream and do!
Come, Presence ever near,
revive us, year by year,
sing through our joy and fear,
Love is making all things new!

Appendix 19

Third Reformed Church Membership Statistics

The membership record of Third Reformed Church at five year intervals as reported in the *Minutes of the General Synod* of the Reformed Church in America.

Year	Number of Families	Members	Friends/ Inactive	Children	Total Members
1870	105	164	[no record]	[nr]	164
1875	151	234	[nr]	[nr]	234
1880	135	250	[nr]	[nr]	250
1885	105	206	[nr]	300	506
1890	140	316	[nr]	480	796
1895	108	298	[nr]	492	790
1900	125	272	[nr]	338	610
1905	150	381	[nr]	[nr]	381
1910	220	526	[nr]	410	936
1915	220	506	50	400	956
1920	255	685	58	260	1,003
1925	428	962	146	318	1,426
1930	387	1,020	177	300	1,497
1935	410	1,044	175	250	1,469
1940	413	928	167	268	1,363
1945	447	990	132	302	1,424
1950	467	890	175	315	1,380
1955	420	809	150	250	1,209
1960	415	788	141	265	1,194
1965	397	768	15	260	1,043
1970	380	810	23	225	1,058
1975	478	817	3	221	1,041
1980	478	818	26	234	1,078
1985	486	899	15	265	1,179
1990	445	753	52	206	1,011
1995	477	766	52	178	996

Appendix 20

Youth Ministers

Roger Rietberg, 1950-1954
Mary Blair Bennett, ?
Phyllis Luidens, ?
Dennis TeBeest, 1976-1977
Todd Van Grouw, 1987-1990
Kevin Hart, 1990-1992
Paul Beauchamp, 1992-

Directors of Christian Education

Elizabeth Koeppe, 1944-1946
Geraldine Smies, 1946-1947
Harold De Roo, 1947-1949
Mark Walvoord, 1967-1974
John Paarlberg, 1974-1978
Kathy Jo Blaske, 1978-1988
Karen Schakel, 1989-

Church Administrator

Karen Schakel, 1990-

Coordinator of Congregational Care

Delores Bechtel, 1993-

Calling Pastors

Rev. Charles Wagner, 1973-1975
Rev. Christian Walvoord, 1978-1979
Rev. Ruth McCarty, 1982-1986
Rev. William Duitsman, 1986
Rev. Glenn Bruggers, 1990-1993

Appendix 21

Is There Any Fight Left in Us?

This sermon, warmly received by many members of the congregation, was preached by the Rev. Dr. Steven S. Stam, in the Third Reformed Church, Holland, Michigan, August 21, 1994.

Text: Ephesians 6:10-20

Not long ago I began to take notice of the fact that few, if any, sermons I preach tell the whole truth. And by that I mean not even the whole truth about any given subject. I find that there is always more to consider—another angle, another perspective, another text, a "what if," a "yes but"—and therefore more that could be said, probably should be said, to correct, to counter-balance, to enlighten. This sermon will be no exception. It will not tell the whole truth. Others can, and probably will, come forward and say, "Yes, but did you consider this?" More truth. Still, I hope we will hear an important truth, a needed truth, nonetheless. I hope we will consider *this.*

The "this" I am talking about is the challenge found in the closing lines of Ephesians. It is familiar material. There has been a lot of traffic through these lines over the years. Less now, I think, than there used to be. For a flannel graph artist, this was the stuff dreams were made of. It was a stirring text for countless baccalaureate sermons and a theme for youth rallies. And, of course, no self-respecting spiralbound songbook published in the 1950s would have dared to bypass this.

But now it has become a troublesome passage, probably for the same reasons which made it a favorite of former generations. I can think of at least two reasons: one because of the metaphors it employs and the other because of the world view it presents. On both counts it seems, if not foreign, at least out of date and, for many of us, downright offensive. It presents a mentality that seems counter-productive to what so many in the church today think we ought to be doing and saying.

These are military metaphors. The church in recent years has made quite an effort to excise such terminology from its working vocabulary. Unlike our forebears, apparently we do not see ourselves, or do not like to see ourselves, as combatants.

I did not chase this down as thoroughly as I would have liked to but I did take the time to look through three successive official hymnbooks of the Reformed Church in America and found in them a total of fourteen hymns with a decidedly militaristic tone to them, with loud, clear, banner-waving, swordbearing, trumpet-blasting, call-to-arms allusions. Hymns like "Onward Christian Soldiers," "The Battle Hymn of the Republic," "Soldiers of Christ, Arise," "Soldiers True and Faithful," "Am I a Soldier of the Cross," "March On, O Soul With Strength," "March to Victory," "The Son of God Goes Forth to War," and "Sound the Battle Cry." There were over a dozen of them in the 1920 hymnal, eight or nine in the 1955 hymnal, and only one, maybe three if you count "A Might Fortress" and the hymn we just sang ("Give me, O Christ, the Strength That Is In Thee") in our current hymnal.

What a row there was in several denominations a decade ago when hymnbook committees tried to quietly omit "Onward Christian Soldiers" from new editions. Now that is the kind of hymn in which you can hear the heels of the combat boots digging in as the Christian soldiers march off to war. I noticed that the Methodists and the Lutherans could not get away with it; they had to keep it in. The old soldiers never die—or even fade away for that matter!

We may wonder what all these military images have to do with the religion of the Prince of Peace. We may be troubled by them and there are plenty of them in the Bible to trouble us. Yet it is precisely because there are so many of them and because they trouble us that we ought to pay attention to them. There is a kind of modern chauvinism that looks back on these ancient texts and back on the hymnody of the previous generations in the smug awareness that we have now advanced beyond all of that. We, at last, are enlightened enough to have found more appropriate ways of expressing ourselves. We will study war no more.

Well, I suppose if there is anything to be said for battlefield metaphors it is that they are graphic, that they get our attention, and that they make their point quite clearly. We can understand this.

I recently went to the video store to rent a copy of *Shadowlands*, the painful story of C. S. Lewis's brief, late-in-life marriage which ended in his wife's death by cancer. I was surprised to learn that only a week after it came out in video it was taken off the new release, two-nights-only rental restriction. Why so soon? I wanted to know. Because not all that many people were asking for it, came the answer. The clerk said it is not like the action-adventure videos which people cannot get enough of. Bombs and blood, that's the formula with the video-renting crowd. Arnold Schwartzeneggar, Sylvester Stallone, Steven Segal, Wesley Snipes. The action may be far-fetched and ridiculous, but people seem to understand it. Ironically, the real gut-wrenching battle of hope and despair, pain and ecstasy, love and loss...well, that sort of gets overlooked. *Shadowlands* could have used some pyrotechnics to illustrate the intensity of the battle.

So maybe the language and images of the battlefield are appropriate after all, if for no other reason than they grab attention and...maybe help to stress the urgency of our business and the importance of what is at stake. The Bible writers knew that. And they knew something else. They knew that there *is* a conflict; there *is* a battle going on and they felt the intensity of that struggle.

Sometimes I think we have lost sight of that. Well, not altogether. We are well aware of the wisdom expressed so succinctly in the bumper sticker proverb: "Life is a struggle...and then you die!" But most of us are primarily occupied with the fight on only one front. There are two. Frederick Buechner, in his book *Magnificent Defeat*, looked at this passage and came away talking about "the two battles."

The first of these, what he calls "a war of conquest," is the one that commands most of our energy and attention and resources. We all fight it. It is a war in the real world against real enemies of flesh and blood. We fight for security, for recognition, for the wherewithal of our livelihood. We fight to have and to hold and to get ahead and stay ahead.

There is quite a lot at stake in this war, a lot for which we will go to the barricades early and often against a variety of contenders. Most of us, especially in this culture, are quite urgent about this and we teach our children to do the same. "Life is a struggle," we tell them, "you have to fight for everything you get." And we arm ourselves to the teeth with the armor with which we have grown accustomed: wit and might and skill and maybe luck or connections or something like that. We will put it on, the whole armor. The battle is real enough, and it keeps us occupied and vigilant pretty much all of the time.

That is one front on which we fight. But there is a second, and it is one of which we seem to be less aware, at least less aware than our forebears. And if not less aware, then less concerned. This is the battle addressed with such urgency here in this passage. And the first thing we are told—and perhaps this is the thing that dulls the reality and the urgency of it in our minds—is that this "struggle" is not against flesh and blood. And the instincts of our modern sophistication says, "Well then, lighten up." This is not the real battle, it is theoretical, maybe symbolic. And we can tuck that one away in some little compartment reserved for special contexts and occasions. After all, it is not the stuff of our everyday lives.

"Our struggle," says the writer of Ephesians, "is...against the rulers, against the authorities, against the cosmic powers of this present darkness, against the spiritual forces of evil in the heavenly places." What is this? I am sure I do not know, but we have every reason to believe that he had a pretty vivid idea of what he was talking about and that there was no doubt in his mind that what he was describing was reality.

It helps me a little bit when I note that what he tells us to arm ourself against is "the wiles of the devil" or more literally, the "methods" of the devil. That is something he believed in as well, and so have a lot of others. If I can refer to C. S. Lewis twice in the same sermon, I would say that he wrote, if not the definitive, at least the classic work on the methods of the devil in his parody, *Screwtape Letters*. Lewis writes:

> There are two equal and opposite errors into which our race can fall about the devils. One is to disbelieve in their existence. The other is to believe, and to feel an excessive and unhealthy interest in them. They themselves are equally pleased by both errors and hail a materialist or a magician with the same delight.

Biblical writers typically saw the devil as a low-key player. That is part of the method. He uses a subtle touch, happy to go unrecognized, happier yet if no one takes him seriously at all. It is like the two boys sitting on the front steps discussing the reality of the devil. "Do you think there is such a thing as the devil?" the one asked. "Naw, not really," the other replied, "Your parents just say that to keep you in line. But I figure he is sort of like Santa Claus; it is really your dad." The devil would be happy with that!

The Apostle says that we "struggle" against this kind of subtle enemy who remains unseen and behind the scenes. Subtle in his methods, but there is nothing subtle about the struggle; it is intentional, fierce, and deadly serious. The Greek word literally means hand-to-hand combat.

We do not know that Paul ever saw combat, but certainly he knew what it was. Roman soldiers were garrisoned everywhere throughout the empire. Everybody knew what they looked like and the weapons with which they fought. Armed as they were, it did not take a lot of imagination to envision the battle. With the exception of a few engineers and archers, combat for most of them was face-to-face, close enough to smell your opponent's breath. It was fearsome, brutal, and horrible in every way.

A week ago I stood with my foot on the stone wall at Cemetery Ridge in Gettysburg, looking across the wheat field, trying to imagine July 3, 1863, and what it was like when the combat reached the hand-to-hand stage, when 6,000 of Pickett's Confederate soldiers were cut down in fifty minutes of the worst imaginable mortal terror. Could this be the sort of thing he had in mind when he said we are locked in a struggle, in hand-to-hand combat, against subtle, unseen forces of evil?

Now, I contrast that struggle with what *I* see. How goes the battle? How intense is it? Is there one? Are you in one? Am I?

This writer in chains can feel the heat. He probably knows something of what it means to "fight wild beasts at Ephesus." The church, as he knows it, is under the gun, and it is a daily fight for survival against ever-present and formidable odds. Ephesus is in Asia, and Asia, as we know from book of Revelation, was a hotbed of imperial persecution. They had all of that to contend with, but worse, far worse, he says, is the battle against the spiritual forces. And besides, he is convinced that whatever there was of physical danger and persecution, it was only the visible outgrowth of the spiritual war, the more profound struggle, against the devil and his minions.

Do you believe that? I don't know; maybe it is easier to talk like that when the more obvious enemies are mounted all around you. Whenever there is some immediate, mortal danger like, say, a war, it is easier to visualize the spiritual forces in the battle. During World War II it did not take much to convince many people that there really was an anti-Christ and he might well be on hand in the person of Hitler. And maybe that is why church attendance and membership in America reached its zenith in the decade following World War II. But when things quiet down and the battle recedes into history, the spiritual struggle does not seem so threatening; it may not seem real at all.

But what if that is when it is most threatening? What if that is the way the enemy's methods work?

Our friend Don Luidens has done much sociological analysis of the church today, and particularly the Reformed Church in America. When we served together on the Regional Synod Executive Council we talked about what it is that threatens the church—and Christians—today. He said, and I agree, that the biggest threat to the church today is leisure. If anything that threatens to kill us, it will be leisure. Leisure may well be what the gates of hell are all about!

Don, as a sociologist, is thinking in terms of the institutional church, something in which I, too, have a great deal of interest. I am thinking more as a pastor and a preacher, thinking beyond the institutional damage to the moral and spiritual threat. How goes the battle? And most people, despite sagging church participation statistics, will look around and say, "What battle?" And maybe with good reason, because, after all, there are not many signs of a struggle.

A good way to measure gains and losses in this battle is by time. It is probably more accurate than measuring real estate as is typical in physical warfare. So measure it in time. Here is family, here is labor, here is leisure, here is the Lord. Now, in the scheduling of your life and the life of your family, look at the columns. Where are the gains and losses over, say, the last ten years? Where is your time going?

How is the church doing in this battle? I have noticed more advertisements for worship services that are scheduled in such a way as not to interfere too much with the other plans we might have for a sunny Sunday. Here is an incident where the whole truth might remind us that this is probably a wonderful idea for reaching out to those who might not otherwise be inclined to visit a worship service. Maybe this will be enough to get them in the door. I am for that. And I certainly do not want to be heard as critical of churches that are adventuresome enough to innovate with something new and creative. But I am talking about church people now, you and me and people like us. I wonder how many of those who attend the mini-service version are those who not long ago were regular in attendance at a worship service that was not scaled down and designed to get you in and out quickly.

When was it that what used to be the Lord's day got reduced to the Lord's hour? How much more can we shorten the program year and cut back and cut out to accommodate everything else until we realize that we are losing the battle? And we are losing the battle because, frankly, most of the time we are not in the battle. In our planning sessions, when we are trying our best to make everything as convenient as possible for everyone, we ought to ask some hard questions about the net effect of all this quest for comfort. We do not want to make any demands, but let me tell you, a battle tends to be a demanding thing. How goes the battle? Time is a pretty good indicator.

Money is another. Look at your check ledger. Morality is another. When Christians lose their moral distinctiveness, when they are unwilling to stand and contend for what is right, we are losing in a big way. Let me ask you, Are your kids growing up with values that are in any way distinctive?

A rabbi from Greenville, North Carolina, is quoted as saying, "We do not trust this place. We do not expect any support or favors. If our kids are going to grow up Jewish, we will have to make them into Jews; nobody will do it for us. So we are always saying to our kind, "That's fine for everybody else, but not for you. You are a Jew."" When was the last time you said that to your son or daughter. "That may be acceptable for someone else, but not for you. You're a Christian."

Many of us were born into a world where Christians seemed secure, confident, and maybe even powerful. That is the way it was with my generation. Growing up in the 1950s around here, our parents worried little about whether or not we would grow up as Christians—it was the only game in town. Everything was closed up on Sundays. Everyone went to church, and Third Church had a thousand in Sunday school. It was American, accepted, the normal thing to do. In that world the church did not have to bother itself too much about defensive maneuvers because, after all, we were fortunate enough to live in a basically Christian country. It was *our* world.

Whether or not our parents really believed this, if you will take a serious look around today, you will find that almost no one believes it anymore. Look around you as you drive to church. More and more of your neighbors are still in their bathrobes. They are sitting this one out. We are on our way to becoming a minority, something we have never been in this town.

Somewhere between 1950 and 1970 the world shifted, and the heat is on once again, even if we do not feel it. No one ought to think that our children will become Christian simply by drinking the water and breathing the air. If our children grow into this faith, we will have to put them there. If we ourselves are going to hold to and live out this faith, we will have to do it with care and determination, with struggle.

The world is giving us fewer and fewer breaks. There will be no government subsidies for the church, no engraved invitations to important state dinners, no free passes to the all-star game. We are not in control anymore—if we ever really were.

Now we have to hold our ground, stand firm, keep our story straight, keep our values clear. The world will defeat or co-opt the weak ones, the ones who have no compelling vision, no armor. We have to abandon a program of adjustment and accommodation. We have to be more intentional about who we are, more careful to give people the equipment they need to discern the true from the false, light from darkness, death from life. We have to get ourselves into the battle.

But we do not go unarmed and we do not go without resources. It is still all there for us, the whole armor or, more literally, the magnificent armor of God. We lack nothing. Stand therefore, Take it up. Put it on. And go.

Best of all, when we go, we do not go alone. He is always to see it through, to see *us* through—all the way. We have his word on that, and that is sufficient.

Appendix 22

The Charter Members of the Third Reformed Church, September 2, 1867

The list is incomplete because the earliest records of the congregation were destroyed in the Fire of 1871. The names of the charter members and their children in this list are taken from the oldest membership record now in existence in the archives of Third Church and from other sources. It appears likely that the oldest membership record of Third Church is the third membership record. According to the handwriting in what is presently the oldest membership record, it can be assumed that it was compiled by the Rev. Henry Dosker during his pastorate, 1889-1894. After he had copied out the information from the second membership record, he apparently disposed of that membership record, which presumbly was compiled after the Holland Fire of 1871. He likely reworked the record begun after the Fire of 1871 because Third Church lost many members during the 1880s due to the Masonic controversy.

Since the names of the first elders and deacons are given in Pastor Dubbink's history of 1899, it was possible to find the names of the entire families in the federal census of Holland City for the year 1870. Gertrude Marsilje Bosman, in her brief history of Third Reformed Church written in 1950, gives the names of the men who were on the building committee and the names of the heads of families. Some of the names of wives and children of these men were also in the 1870 census.

Final determination of this charter membership list is, therefore, dependent on four sources primarily: the supposed third membership record of Third Church [c.1890], names of men in the Bosman history, the Dubbink history, and the 1870 federal census. Unfortunately, no mention was made of departing members from the First Reformed Church [the records of which church are located at the Pillar Christian Reformed Church] when Third Reformed Church was organized in 1867.

According to the Rev. Dr. Gerrit H. Dubbink, author of the first history of the church, 267 men, women, and children were charter members of which number, fifty-five men and forty-two women were communicant members. This list numbers 234 men, women, and children.

Since the earliest membership record often gives birthdates, those dates follow most of the individuals' names. Dates of birth may help those interested in genealogy.

It can be assumed that the abbreviation "Ma" in the membership record stands for March because the recorder writes "May" out in full.

This membership record of Third Church often lists more children for the charter members than were living in 1867 because the list was compiled during the later 1880s. However, only children's names are listed here if the children were born before the organization of the congregation on September 2, 1867. Anyone interested in genealogical information on a given family may consult this record, which, by the way, is on microfilm in the Herrick Public Library in Holland, Michigan.

Baas, Willem, Ma[r]. 16, 1827
Margaretha de Vries, Ma[r]. 15, 1831
Antje [Anna], Feb. 13, 1853
Willem, Feb. 4, 1856
Barent, Nov. 24, 1858
Nellie [Neltje], June 21, 1860
Grietje, July 30, 1861
Guurtje, Apr. 1, 1862
Ida, Nov. 22, 1863
Katie, Sept. 8, 1866
[The family emigrated from Zaandam, the Netherlands, in August, 1856. All of the children were baptized by A. C. Van Raalte, as were many of the children in this list.]

Bennink, Harmina, Jan. 25, 1820

Boot, Pieter, Ma[r]. 13, 1852

Borgers, Johanna, May 21, 1851 [She married Pieter de Vries (born Sept. 24, 1843), who united with the church June 1, 1884.]

Bruisgaat, Abraham
Geisje van der Kamp
Abram, May 9, 1860
Johannes, Jan. 8, 1863

Cappon, Isaac, Jan. 30, 1830
Catarina de Boe, Jan. 5, 1835
Magdalena Cornelia, Jan. 15, 1855
Cornelia M., Sept. 15, 1856
Elizabeth M., Sept. 11, 1858
John J., Sept. 13, 1860
Jacobus M., Dec. 25, 1862
Cornelia, Ma[r]. 28, 1867
Mina, Aug. 28, 1867
[The compiler of this church record apparently was very proud that the Cappon family was in Third Church. The family was the first one listed in this church record!]

Clonz, Jan, June 20, 1830
[no wife was listed, but the son, Joost, was born Oct. 2, 1867, shortly after Third Church was organized.]
Kaatje, June 2, 1864

Daalman, Geert, Aug. 28, 1831
Anna Maria Voorst, Feb. 22, 1840
Maria Katherina, Dec. 27, 1866

de Boer, Simon
Hendrika Hoekstra
Jenny de Boer (Jansje) Sept. 27, 1862, [baptized in Vriesland, Michigan, by the Rev. Adrian Zwemer.]

De Bruyn, Robbertus M.
Susana
Peter
Robert
John

de Jong, Cornelis, May 2, 1821
Heiltje Schaap, (widow of Plugger), June 8, 1826

de Vries, Hendrikus, Jan. 5, 1818
Adriana de Kok, Nov. 16, 1820
Tryntje (Kate), Oct. 5, 1853
Jacob, Nov. 14, 1856
Johanna and Eltje, Nov. 19, 1857
Pieter, June 6, 1860
Nelltje, June 17, 1863

de Weert, Wympje Van de Vusse, Oct. 9, 1818, widow
Jan, Nov. 29, 1857

Diekema, Wiepke, Dec. 28, 1830
Hendrikje Stegeman, May 2, 1826
Hendrika, Ma[r]. 25, 1854
Pieter, Sept. 16, 1856
Gerrit Jan, Ma[r]. 27, 1859*
Eldert, Ma[r]. 15, 1861
Winnie Catherina, May 11, 1863
Albert, Sept. 13, 1865
Martha, Apr. 21, 1867+

*Gerrit J. Diekema was minister plenipoteniary of the United States to the Netherlands at the time of his death in 1930. He and his wife built the home which now serves as the parsonage of Third Church.
+Martha Diekema Kollen was the donor of Kollen Park which is located on the west side of the city of Holland.

Elferdink, Willem, Ma[r]. 5, 1841
Hendrika Uiterwijk, Oct. 22, 1843
Johanna Aleida, Apr. 2, 1866

Everhard, Evert, Feb. 16, 1818
Hendrika Gerridina Brinkerhoff, Feb. 21, 1824
Jan Dirk, Jan. 22, 1845
Aleida Beredina, Feb. 8, 1847
Everdina Cornelia, June 3, 1853
Albertus Bernardus

Kerkhof, Jan Martinus, Aug. 25, 1824

Roeltje van Lente, Nov. 2, 1829
Cornelia, Feb. 9, 1858 [it is likely 1848, not 1858]
Maria, Feb. 4, 1853
Jan, Nov. 25, 1855
Frederika Maria, Apr. 10, 1858
Cornelia, Ma[r]. 25, 1860
Frederik, Dec. 25, 1861
Johanna Hendrika, Feb. 10, 1863

Kieft, F[rederick]
Ella W.
Willem
Jaantje
Bernardus

Koning, Jacobus, Nov. 8, 1832 [he made confession of faith, Ma[r] 13, 1887]
Gezina Albers, Nov. 9, 1832
Gerrit, July 28, 1856
John, Feb. 27, 1858
James, Sept. 10, 1860
Pieter, Apr. 10, 1862
Nellie Maria, Jan. 2, 1865
Nellie Maria, July 2, 1867

Labots, Jacob
Mary

Lindeweg, Loentje Adolphina (widow of Hubrecht vande Berg), Jan. 23, 1822

Nibbelink, Jacobus Hendrikus, Feb. 21, 1835
Gesina Pessink [The record is clear that she united with Third in 1867 but it does not mention his becoming a member in full communion. Their three children who were born in 1870, 1873, and 1877 were all baptized at Third.]

Nibbelink, Wesselius Casparus, Dec. 18, 1837
Elizabeth Van Engen, Dec. 20, 1838
Wesselius Casparus, May 15, 1863
Dirk [listed as Albertus in the 1870 census], July 3, 1865
Berdine Hendrina, July 7, 1867

Paules, John
Johanna
Arie
Otto
Mary
Albert
Anthony
Maalke

Prakken, Jan, Sept. 5, 1837
Cornelia Cats, Oct. 27, 1837
Nikalos [Klaas], Aug. 20, 1866

Scholz [s], Cornelis Hendrik, Feb. 7, 1826
Tietje Dykstra, Jan. 11, 1826
Cornelis
Conraad
Gezina

Slooter, Pieter, Nov. 6, 1834
Dina de Boe, Nov. 19, 1840 [a sister of Mrs. Isaac Cappon]
Adriana, Ma[r]. 25, 1862
Cornelia, Apr. 3, 1864
Adrianus, Sept. 3, 1866

[Peter Slooter was listed as a tanner in the Holland Directory of 1894; a son born, Ma[r]. 7, 1879, was named Isaac Cappon Slooter.]

Sprietsma, Simon Lucas, Apr. 15, 1845
Geertruida Wilhelmina Elferdink, Aug. 11, 1842
Lucas, July 31, 1864
Hannah, Feb. 18, 1866

Te Roller, Derk
Hendrika
Henry
Hannah+
Maria

Dirk
Reka [Hendrika]
+Hannah was the first organist of Third Church.

Te Vaarrock, G. J.
Grietje
Hendrika
Pieter
William
Trimpe, Jan Wilmina

Uiterwijk, Hendrikus, July 6, 1811
[His daughter, Hendrika, was the wife of Willem Elferdink, and they were charter members of Third Church. See the Elferdink listing above.]
[It is not known if Hendrikus Uiterwijk was a relative of the Rev. Henry Uiterwijk [Utterwick], second pastor of Third Church.]

Van Ark, Gerardus, Nov. 3, 1836
Aaltje Oldenhof, May 10, 1830
Aaltje, Aug. 17, 1863

van Dam, Jan, Nov. 4, 1834
Geertruida Van Lente, Sept. 10, 1832
Fannetje, Ma[r]. 13, 1856
Maria, Oct. 15, 1857
Adriana, Aug. 4, 1859
Frederika, June 18, 1861
Cornelis, Sept. 16, 1862
Adriana, May 28, 1864
Frederika Johanna, Dec. 11, 1866

Van Der Haar, Hein [Henry], Nov. 25, 1821
Maria Geertruida Brummelaar, June 23, 1845
Jan, Sept. 13, 1866

Van der Veen, Engbertus, Apr. 1, 1828
Tantje Verbeek, Oct. 20, 1832
Jacob, Sept. 19, 1854
Cornelia Jacoba, Aug. 12, 1856
Cornelia Jacoba, Nov. 21, 1857

Anna Gertrude, June 22, 1859
Derk Edward, Ma[r]. 13, 1861
Engbertus Arent, Sept. 23, 1861
Willem Cornelis Jacobus, Feb. 7, 1864
Cornelia Jacoba, Apr. 26, 1866

[Since there were three daughters named Cornelia Jacoba, it can be assumed that the first two so named died in early childhood and were not living on Sept. 2, 1867. Father Engbertus was a successful Holland businessman, a tinsmith, whose business was located at 8th Street and River Ave. He fabricated the rooster weathervane which is still atop the Pillar Christian Reformed Church.]

Van der Veer, Cornelis, Dec. 18, 1811
Pietertje
Catharina
Bowke
Cornelis
Elle
William

Van Dyk, Jan, Nov. 5, 1838
Martine de Fuyter, Jan. 16, 1849
Aaltje Elizabeth, Feb. 4, 1867

Van Dyk, Teunis, Ma[r]. 23, 1832
Maria Teeselink, Aug. 26, 1833
Albert, Ma[r]. 9, 1858
Henry Alfred, Jan. 6, 1861
Johannes, Apr. 14, 1863
Willem Edward, June 4, 1865

Van Dyke, Jan, July 7, 1808
Jacob, Ma[r]., 1835
Elizabeth, June 29, 1837

Van Heruynen, Cornelis

Van Lente, Berent Lambertus, Sept. 2, 1824
Wilhelmina Baarsches, Feb. 21, 1829
Maria, Apr. 7, 1850

Johanna, June 15, 1852
Frederika, July 15, 1855
Geertruida, Feb. 6, 1857
Hattie, May 6, 1859
Frederik, Apr. 28, 1861
Maria Geertruida, Dec. 28, 1863
John, Ma[r]. 12, 1865
Bert, May 8, 1867

Van Zee, Eppink

Verbeek, Willem, Feb. 16, 1837
Fanna Zaalmink, Oct. 21, 1839

Verhulst, Antoni
Maatje
Johannes, Feb. 9, 1849
Arnold, Nov. 21, 1857
Cornelis
Martha

Visscher, Arend, Oct. 3, 1849

Visscher, Jan Family

Werkman, D. Family

Werkman, E.
Geertje W. Bolling, Aug. 12, 1820
Aafke[?], Apr. 29, 1843
Wisberdina, Jan. 13, 1845
Geertruida, May 18, 1849
Elizabeth, Nov. 25, 1850
Jan, Feb. 23, 1852
Antje, Jan. 28, 1853
Reinder, June 24, 1855
Jenny, Nov. 12, 1857
Hattie, Dec. 11, 1859
Annie, June 10, 1862

Effie, Apr. 21, 1865

Winter, Eije, Ma[r]. 9, 1829
Frederika Berendina Smits, Aug. 3, 1839
Rienie Pieternella, Nov. 4, 1866

Winter, Pieter, July 9, 1824
Anje Bolhuis, Jan. 3, 1834
Rena (Rientje), June 12, 1855
Betsy (Bowke), July 30, 1859
Annie [Anna], July 7, 1863

Zuidema, David
Margaret
Frances
Nancy
Albert

Endnotes

Chapter 1

1. Then known as Market Street.
2. For the background information on the immigrants in the Netherlands I am indebted to the work of Henry S. Lucas, whose masterful *Netherlanders in America*, (Ann Arbor: University of Michigan Press, 1955), is a classic in the field. A definitive work on the events preceding the Secession of 1834 is *Sources of Secession: The Netherlands Hervormde Kerk on the Eve of the Dutch Immigration to the Midwest*, by Gerrit J. ten Zythoff (The Historical Series of the Reformed Church in America, No. 17. Wm. B. Eerdmans Publishing Co., Grand Rapids, Michigan, 1987).
3. Lucas, op. cit., pp. 49-50.
4. Quoted by Lucas, ibid. p. 93.
5. "Life Reminiscences of Engbertus Vander Veen," a member of Third Church, relate with poignancy the great hardships of those days. *Dutch Immigrant Memoirs and Related Writings*, (Assen, the Netherlands: Van Gorcum and Company, 1955), edited by Henry S. Lucas, Vol. I, pp. 489-514.
6. "The Pillar Church" and the First Reformed Church were synonymous until 1882, when the majority of the congregation seceded from the Reformed Church in America. In 1884, the seceders affiliated with the Christian Reformed Church and the Pillar Church congregation was renamed the Ninth Street

Christian Reformed Church. The congregation is now called the Pillar Christian Reformed Church.

7. *Classis Holland, Minutes*, 1848-1858 (Wm. B. Eerdmans Publishing Company, Grand Rapids, Michigan, 1950), p. 18.
8. Ibid., pp. 36-37.
9. The Central Avenue Christian Reformed Church.
10. *Minutes, General Synod*, 1867, p. 209.
11. *A Brief Historical Sketch of the Third Reformed Church, Holland, Michigan* (Holland, Michigan: Ottawa County Times Presses, 1899), Gerrit H. Dubbink, p. 6. The pamphlet is a concise and indispensable record of the early years of Third Church. Dubbink was pastor of the church at the time he wrote this account and undoubtedly learned much from charter members who were still living.
12. The first minute book of Third Church was burned in the Holland Fire of 1871.
13. Translation by Dr. Wynand Wichers.
14. Now called the First United Methodist Church.
15. Grace Episcopal Church.
16. Dubbink, *op. cit.*, p. 6. Since it was a Dutch custom to give the initial of the first name only, a custom which Dr. Dubbink is following in his history of Third Church, the author of this history has learned of many first names primarily through the Holland census of 1870. The one uncertainty regarding the first names of these individuals is that of Frederick Kieft. It is likely that his first name is Frederick but that is uncertain. See appendix 22 for a fairly complete listing of other charter members of the Third Reformed Church.

Chapter 2

1. "The Burning of Holland," *Dutch Immigrant Memoirs and Related Writings* (Van Gorcum & Company N.V., 1955), vol. II, p. 1.
2. *Holland Daily Evening Sentinel*, August 25, 1897.
3. Gerrit Van Schelven, op. cit., vol. II, p. 2.
4. Ibid.
5. The low amount of insurance coverage may be due to the fact that many immigrants thought that having insurance was tempting Providence and showed a lack of Christian faith.
6. Van Schelven, op.cit., p. 5. The only item of Third Church not lost in the fire was the pulpit Bible which was rescued by a young man, George Dalman.
7. Not everyone was sympathetic to Holland's plight. Van Schelven reported that some people said:

> The Hollanders refused to aid in extinguishing the fire for the reason that it was Sunday, and that the churches would not permit their bells to be rung, fearing it would disturb the congregation.

The Hollanders were known apparently for their observance of the Sabbath but this report was untrue. Ibid., p. 6

8. *Historical Celebration Souvenir, Third Reformed Church*, 1917, p. 9. During Utterwick's ministry at Third Church, he used his original name, "Uiterwijk." After he left Holland, he Americanized his name to Utterwick and was known by the name of Utterwick for most of his life. He died in Rutherford, New Jersey, in 1928.
9. *Holland City News*, January 4, 1873, p. 3.
10. The home at 121 West 12th Street, across the street from Third Church, was also constructed from the timbers of the framework that had blown down, according to Dale and Ann Van Lente who had lived in this home at one time.
11. *Historical Celebration Souvenir*, p. 9.
12. Ibid.
13. *Holland City News*, November 28, 1874, p. 4.
14. Ibid.
15. Ibid. Dr. Donald J. Bruggink, in a brochure written for the "open house" of Third Reformed Church, June 16, 1968, said:

> The nineteenth century witnessed a revival of Gothic architecture. Richard Upjohn completed the present Trinity Church on Wall Street in 1846. It was widely admired as the most handsome church in America and was widely imitated not only in stone, but in brick and wood as well. Third Church is a handsome and aesthetically pleasing variant of this nineteenth century Gothic known as carpenters' Gothic. Certain detailing in the interior columns and arches can be found in another famous church of Richard Upjohn, St. Paul's Church in Buffalo, New York, completed in 1851.

16. Dubbink, op.cit., pp. 11-12.
17. A report in the *Holland City News*, September 12, 1874.
18. The *Holland City News* reported on December 26, 1874, that "We are not wanting in singing societies." Mr. C. Van Oostenbrugge conducted a choral group which met every Thursday evening in the

consistory room of Third Church. There was a musical group at the college. The choir of First Reformed Church rehearsed on Monday evenings, the choir of Third on Tuesday evenings, led by C. De Jong, and the True Reformed Church (Central Avenue Christian Reformed Church) even had a choir which rehearsed on Thursday evenings. The colony had taken to music.

19. B[ernardus] DeBey and A[drian] Zwemer, *Stemmen Uit de HollandschGereformeerde Kerk* (Groningen: G. J. Reets, 1871), pp. 118-19.
20. *One Hundred[sic] Anniversary Historical Booklet*, First Reformed Church, Holland, Michigan, 1947, p. 12.
21. Quoted by Gerrit Van Schelven in his essay, "The Second Revival," January, 1913. Located in the archives of the Holland Museum, the Joint Archives Collections, Van Wylen Library, Hope College.
22. Quoted by Henry Lucas, *Netherlanders in America*, p. 61.
23. Ibid., p. 601.
24. Ibid.
25. *Holland City News*, May 2, 1874.
26. Lucas, op.cit., p. 589.
27. *Holland City News*, September 27, 1879, p. 1.
28. See the appendix for a list of Third Church members who served on the school board. A handbill distributed in 1920 protested publicly that Third Church had three members running for the school board. The handbill is found in the archives of the Holland Museum at the Joint Archives, Hope College.
29. See my study of Cappon, entitled, "Isaac Cappon: Holland's 'Foremost Citizen,'" 1987. Printed privately. Cappon's influence touched the religious, educational, and business life of the Holland community.
30. After the death of his daughter, Lavina, in 1978, the City of Holland purchased the home. It is now a historical museum.
31. *Holland City News*, August 7, 1880.
32. The archives of the City of Holland, the Holland Museum collection, the Joint Archives, Hope College.
33. Her baptized name was Magdalena.

Chapter 3

1. For a detailed study of the Masonic controversy, see my essay, entitled, "The Masonic Controversy in Holland, Michigan, 1879-1882" in *Perspectives on the Christian Reformed Church: Studies in Its History, Theology and Ecumenicity*, Peter de Klerk and

Richard R. Ridder, editors. (Grand Rapids: Baker Book House, 1983), pp. 53-72.

2. A quote by Henry E. Dosker, in his biography of Van Raalte, entitled, *Levensschets van Rev. A. C. Van Raalte, D.D.* (Nijkerk: C. C. Callenbach, 1893), p. 331.
3. Nicholas Dosker, *De Hollandsche Gereformeerde Kerk in Amerika* (Nijmegen: P. J. Milborn, 1888), p. 207.
4. June 7, 1879, p. 4.
5. *Holland City News*, July 12, 1879, p. 4.
6. Minutes of the Consistory, August 29, 1879.
7. Although the Classis of Holland took an anti-Masonic stance, Third Church accepted Masons into its membership eventually, but, until the 1930s, it was understood that lodge members could not be elected to the consistory.
8. *Historical Celebration Souvenir*, p. 17.
9. Ibid., p. 16.
10. Ibid., p. 17.
11. Vol. I, no. 1, p. 2.
12. Dubbink, op.cit., p. 24.
13. Henry E. Dosker, *Historical Celebration Souvenir*, p. 18.
14. Dubbink, op.cit., p. 25.
15. Ibid., p. 26.
16. *Fiftieth Anniversary of the Fourth Reformed Church, 1896-1946*, p. 5.
17. *The Holland Evening Sentinel*, May 15, 1937.
18. The Classis of Michigan was organized in 1841. The first congregations of this classis were Grand Rapids (later known as the First Reformed Church which later merged with the Second Reformed Church in 1918 and is now called the Central Reformed Church), Centreville, Constantine, Ridgeway, Allegan, and Redford. Edward Tanjore Corwin, *A Digest of Constitutional and Synodical Legislation of the Reformed Church in America* [Formerly the Ref. Prot. Dutch Church] (New York: The Board of Publication of the Reformed Church in America, 1906), p. 387.

Chapter 4

1. *The Telegraph*, July, 1903. Date unknown.
2. Information from Dr. J. Dyke Van Putten, Professor of Political Science at Hope College (1952-1969), who was attending the Fourteenth Street Christian Reformed Church at the time of the controversy.
3. *The Bulletin*, July 14, 1918.
4. *The Financial Report*, 1913.
5. Aleida J. Pieters, *A Dutch Settlement in Michigan* (Grand Rapids, Michigan: The Reformed Press, 1923), p. 126.
6. An original copy of the program

is in the Joint Archives of Holland, the Van Wylen Library, Hope College. The story of the event was written by Samuel M. Zwemer, entitled, *The Ship That Sailed and a Keel That Never Kissed the Sea*, 1931.

7. Arend Visscher, *Historical Celebration Souvenir*, p. 1.
8. Pieters, op. cit., p. 128.
9. *Historical Celebration Souvenir*, p. 40.
10. Pastor Blekkink followed his predecessors, Dosker and Dubbink, to Western Theological Seminary in 1912. Dr. Dosker served at Western Seminary as professor of church history, 1895-1903, and concluded his career in the same field at the Louisville Presbyterian Seminary, 1903-1926. Dr. Dubbink had served as professor of theology, 1904-1910, the year of his premature death. Dr. Blekkink was professor of theology, 1912-1928. The widow of Dr. Dubbink, Margaret Kollen Dubbink, and Evert and Hattie Blekkink remained life-long members of Third Church. The children of the Blekkinks, Ruth and Victor, established an endowed professorship at Hope College in their parents' honor in 1980. Members of Third Church, Elton Bruins and Dennis Voskuil, held the Blekkink Chair, 1980-1992 and 1992-1994, respectively. Dr. Voskuil resigned the position in 1994 when he assumed the presidency of Western Theological Seminary.

Chapter 5

1. The Michigan Classis was comprised of Reformed church congregations which never used Dutch in the worship services, like Hope Reformed Church in Holland. Churches such as the First Reformed Church of Grand Rapids, which had been founded in 1840, were formed by Dutch Reformed church members who had migrated from New York and New Jersey to Michigan before the Dutch migration to Michigan which began in 1847. After the Dutch immigrant churches all began to use English, classis boundaries were realigned and the Michigan Classis ceased to exist. Another cause for the dissolution of the Michigan Classis was that most of its churches went out of existence in the process of time.
2. Charter members were Clarence Klaasen, Nelson Bosman, Nelson Karsten, Harold DuMez, Neal Zeerip, Arthur Beekman, Edward Dekker, Cornelius Van Dyke, John Zeerip, Gerald Bolhuis, Earl Slagh, and Paul Nettinga.

William C. Eby was the scout master. The Bulletin, May 22, 1921.

3. August 14, 1921.
4. The four-volume work has been reissued in 1994 by the Baker Book House of Grand Rapids. Reuben A. Torrey was one of the editors. The ministers in the Reformed Church in America who contributed to this series were George Sayles Bishop and David James Burrell. Burrell was pastor of the Marble Collegiate Church at the time he contributed to the series of essays which comprise this publication. Daniel Hoffman Martin also contributed an essay. He no longer was a pastor of the Reformed Church in America, however, joining the Presbyterian Church a few years prior to the publication. See Catherine L. Albanese, *America Religions and Religion* (Belmont, California: Wadsworth Publishing Company, 1981), pp. 103ff. for more information on the Fundamentalist movement.
5. *The Bulletin*, October 1, 1922.
6. *The Bulletin*, June 13, 1926.
7. The congregation of Third Church still has a tie with both James Zwemer and Siebe Nettinga. They are the grandfather and father respectively of Cornelia Nettinga Neevel, a longtime member of the congregation.
8. *Minutes of the General Synod*, 1924, p. 635.
9. It is of interest to note that immediately upon the death of Arend Visscher in 1921, his widow and children transferred their membership to the Hope Reformed Church.
10. Henry Geerlings was also a leader in the Holland community, serving as mayor in the early 1940s. "50 Years Ago Today, March 19, 1942," *The Holland Sentinel*, Sunday, March 15, 1992, p. F5 and "50 Years Ago Today April 17, 1944," *The Holland Sentinel*, Sunday, April 17, 1994, p. F6.
11. *The Bulletin*, July 29, 1917.
12. January 28, 1923.
13. Between 1893-1923, or thirty years. He continued as songleader in the Sunday school until 1943, having served Third Church for fifty years in some phase of Third's music program.
14. December 11, 1903.
15. This organ was rebuilt by the Austin Company for a Roman Catholic church in Indiana.
16. He served as president of Hope College from 1893 to 1911.
17. *The Bulletin*, November 20, 1927.
18. The chapel is now known as the Dimnent Memorial Chapel which was dedicated in 1929.
19. "Classical appointments" was a system of the classis whereby

installed ministers would be assigned to preach occasionally in churches in the classis who were without pastors. The system assisted small or struggling congregations which may have been without pastors for extended lengths of time. In the very early days of the Holland churches, elders would conduct services and read sermons from an approved published sermon collection. Although the system of classical appointments is still in use in some parts of the Reformed Church in America, Holland Classis gave up the practice, possibly due to the ready supply of professors and students at Western Seminary.

20. There was at that time the "long" and the "short" form of the communion liturgy. Because of the extreme length of the "long" form, most congregations used the "short" form.
21. This unfortunate term is still in use in the Reformed church. It leaves the impression that a congregation is functioning only when an installed minister is serving the church. It casts a negative impression that lay people are not as valuable as the ordained, installed pastor.
22. When Dr. Oudersluys was called to the New Testament chair at Western Seminary in 1942 and moved to Holland, he and his family joined Third Church.
23. March 15, 1925.
24. *The Bulletin*, October 13, 1940.

Chapter 6

1. *Historical Directory of the Reformed Church in America, 1628-1992*, Russell L. Gasero, editor (Grand Rapids, Michigan: Wm. B. Eerdmans Publishing Co., 1992), pp. 333-34.
2. From 1896 to 1946, the windows consisted of an art glass purchased from the Carson Art Glass Works of Chicago, at a total cost of $229.50, or $14 per window (*The Bulletin*, August 7, 1921). The only remaining sample of this period is the large window on the north end of the sanctuary.
3. The grandmother of Steven De Young, a current member of the congregation.
4. *The Bulletin*, November 30, 1955.
5. Now called the Dimnent Memorial Chapel.
6. After the Peale Science Center was completed in 1973, the old science building was converted into a classroom building for the Humanities and Social Science classes and renamed Lubbers Hall in honor of the former president Irwin Lubbers and his wife, Margaret.
7. Now called Vander Werf Hall in honor of former president,

Calvin A. Vander Werf.

8. Unfortunately, the Riverford Heights congregation was disbanded in 1967.
9. In a letter to the members of Third Church, February 7, 1928, Geerlings said:

   I am greatly indebted to the members of our church for the expression of their good will and confidence in my election to the consistory. I also appreciated the delicate situation of the present moment. The church is greater than any individual or group of individuals.

   We cannot afford to have any friction. The church is the biggest organization in our world and to do effective work we must stand together.

   In view of all this I feel it my duty to decline the eldership.

10. St. Nicholas Church was a member church of the Collegiate Church of New York, a system which was modeled on the Dutch Reformed Church structure in the Netherlands. The best known church in the Collegiate Church system was the Marble Collegiate Church, pastored by Norman Vincent Peale at that time. The collegiate churches on Manhattan Island date from 1628 when the first Dutch Reformed Church minister, Jonas Michaelius, came to Manhattan to serve the Dutch immigrants. The Reformed Church in America uses this date as the founding of the denomination also.
11. From a letter to Dr. Donald J. Bruggink, written August 12, 1965, shortly before Dr. Sizoo's death. However, the letter was not mailed at that time but was later found among Dr. Sizoo's papers by his secretary, Dolores N. Bedford, who forwarded it to Dr. Bruggink. In the letter, Sizoo commented, "I am glad that the chancel furniture is used by your church. I worshipped in your church when I was a college student at Hope. There is, therefore, something both sentimental and poignant to me about the fact that you use it."
12. Much of this material on worship at Third Church is adapted from a brochure written by Donald Bruggink and Elton Bruins for the "open house" celebration, June 16, 1968.

Chapter 7

1. The crusade began on Memorial Day and ended on Labor Day.
2. For references on the movement see *God's Spirit Among Us* by Dennis Bennett, 1974; *The Charismatic Movement* by Michael P. Hamilton, 1975; and *They Speak*

in Other Tongues by John J. Sherrill, 1964.

3. *Christianity Today*, September 2, 1983, pp. 33-36. The term "refers to acts by Christians who either engage only in 'believer's baptism' or promote analogous experiences among the 'baptismally regenerate,' for example through Pentecostal 'second baptisms' or 'second blessings,'" p. 33.
4. See *American Mainline Religion: Its Changing Shape and Future*, by Wade Clark Roof and William McKinney for a full discussion of the term (Rutgers University Press, 1987).
5. The movement was a separation from the Hervormde Kerk or State Church. The Rev. Albertus C. Van Raalte was a minister in the Afscheiding before migrating to America in 1846 and founding Holland, Michigan, on February 9, 1847. See chapter one for more details.
6. *The Church Herald*, May 9, 1969, p. 5.
7. "Special Education Ministry Marks 20th Anniversary," *The Holland Sentinel*, April 23, 1988, p. C5.
8. "Special Education Ministries Celebrates 25th" in *The Holland Sentinel*, April 23, 1993. "Special Education Ministries, a dream, now a reality," by Amy Kortering appeared in *The Holland Sentinel* on October 29, 1993, p. C1. Note that the name of the program was changed from Special Education Ministry to Special Education Ministries between 1988 and 1993.
9. Tom Arendshorst, Deb Sterken, and Bob Carlson.
10. For instance, in March of 1991, a bulletin insert reported to the congregation that the Good Samaritan Center wished to thank Third Church for its support during 1990: for $625 contributed as a congregation in addition to $1,500 contributed by individual members of the congregation; for financial assistance to three families; for Thanksgiving baskets for four families; for Christmas gifts to two handicapped individuals; for use of the Third Church van and of Jim Ver Hulst, Third's custodian, as driver to transport dental clients; for Jon Bechtel's work as Good Samaritan Center's contact person with Third; for Pastor Ron Franklyn's effective help to those with alcohol problems and referral to AA; for Norma Killilea's coordination of fifteen nurses to staff the Buen Pastor migrant day care center; for Deb Sterken's serving as president of the Villa Aurora Task Force; and for Kathi Bates's contribution as an outstanding board member.

11. "The Third Reformed Church Newsletter," January, 1973, p. 1. The first chairperson was Elton Bruins. Historical note: this newsletter was instituted just before Pastor Vande Bunte concluded his ministry at Third Church. The newsletter, which serves as the prime source of information about the life and activity of Third Church, had no formal name until it was called *The Third Generation* in August, 1980. Two complete sets of the newsletters since 1969 are in the church archives.
12. Information on the back of a church bulletin under the heading, "The Christian Action Council of the Third Reformed Church."
13. CROP stands for the Christian Rural Overseas Program, a community hunger appeal program of Church World Service. *The Third Generation*, May, 1983, p. 1.
14. *The Third Generation*, November, 1984, p. 11.
15. *The Third Generation*, May, 1991, pp. 1-2.
16. *The Third Generation*, September, 1982, p. 2.
17. *The Third Generation*, March, 1986, p. 2.
18. Third Church *Bulletin* insert, April 28, 1991.
19. This program was in cooperation with Channel Ministries, a local Reformed church work, and Habitat for Humanity. Third Church *Bulletin* insert, May 3, 1992.
20. *The Third Generation*, May, 1992, p. 6.
21. The Roger Rietberg file, Third Church archives.
22. The Third Church *Bulletin*, June 15, 1986.
23. Unfortunately, there was no recognition of Miss Schuppert's work in the first printing of the new hymnbook. Her name did appear in the later printings.
24. This hymnbook has not been well regarded in the churches of the denomination because it is deemed too difficult for the average congregation and devoid of many familiar hymns. Only eight percent of Reformed Church in America congregations use this hymnbook, a statistic reported in a newsletter from the RCA Office for Worship, April, 1994. Since Third Church is blessed with an excellent organist and adult choir, the congregation has the leadership to appreciate the good qualities of this hymnbook.
25. Minutes of the consistory, June 8, 1976, as quoted in the June, 1977, church newsletter.
26. Elder Elaine Jekel, when reviewing the second draft of chapter seven, wrote: "The arguments to the congregation in proposing two morning services were that the large

crowd demanded this in order to accommodate everyone. Each October, in particular, there were not enough seats even with the many additional chairs in the back. At the congregational meeting at the time of the vote, it was pointed out that we would need two services even without a new organ. The beginning of the two services occurred several months before the installation of the new organ. Lyle Schaller articles were widely studied. To attract new people for membership, empty pews must be visible. Willis Jones and the Administrative and Personnel Committee wanted to make sure that the two morning services were not related to the organ's arrival."

27. A booklet was prepared for the dedication with a letter by Pastor Jones; "A Historical Note on the Organs of the Third Reformed Church, 1883 to 1982," by Elton Bruins; and "The Sipe Organ" by Roger Rietberg.
28. In a full report on the proposed new organ, Jon Bechtel made a spirited defense for obtaining a new instrument. Canceling the contract at that time would have involved a considerable loss of funds since a contract already had been signed. *The Third Generation*, September, 1980, pp. 5-8.
29. The strategic planning program went by the name "MasterPlan." No space between the two words is intentional.
30. *Minutes of the General Synod*, 1972, pp.119-20.
31. RCW is currently known as RCWM, Reformed Church Women's Ministries.
32. As reported in the Third Church *Newsletter*, August, 1979, p. 5.
33. For full accounts of this event, see the Third Church *Newsletter* for March, 1973, pp. 5 and 6 and the April edition, p. 7.
34. The Third Church *Newsletter*, March, 1976, pp. 1 and 2.
35. The Third Church *Bulletin*, October 31, 1976. The information was presented as follows: "Four octaves of our set of Schulmerich Bells have arrived, the gift of Mr. Henry Du Mez and his sister, Mrs. Walter Frei, in memory of Mr. and Mrs. Gerrit Du Mez, Miss Bertha Du Mez, and Mrs. Henry Du Mez. A few of the bells are on display in the library and can be seen during the coffee hour following morning worship. We are very grateful for this generous gift which will be an enrichment of our services of worship."
36. *The Third Generation*, April, 1984, pp. 1-3.
37. *The Third Generation*, September, 1984, pp. 6-7. The first session was held on

September 9.

38. Pp. 1-3.
39. It must also be noted that many persons have transferred from Christ Memorial Church to Third Church during the same period. When twenty-one new persons were received into the membership of Third Church on November 14, 1993, seven of them came from Christ Memorial.
40. Excerpts from the official records of Third Church relating to the conclusion of Pastor Roorda's ministry are as follows:

    Elders' meeting, January 14, 1990: "A discussion was held around the questions: Are there issues? What issues? What do we do?...A motion was made to send a delegation of three to counsel the Rev. Roorda as to the situation and request a response from him within two weeks. Motion carried unanimously. Elder Beth Marcus, Elder Donald Cronkite and Deacon Harvey Buter will meet with the Rev. Roorda.

    Consistory meeting, January 16, 1990: No mention is made in the minutes of the January 14 meeting of the elders. Pastor Roorda was congratulated upon the acceptance of his dissertation for the Doctor of Ministry degree at San Francisco Theological Seminary.

    Special consistory meeting, January 20, 1990: "After sharing some comments about the developments of the past week, Rev. Roorda distributed and read a letter of resignation as the Senior Pastor of the Third Reformed Church. A discussion between Rev. Roorda and the Consistory members followed....A motion was made to accept the resignation of the Senior Pastor; and to refer to the Administration and Personnel Committee negotiations for the timing and the severance arrangements returning a proposal to the Consistory for approval."

    Special consistory meeting, January 30, 1994: "Dr. [David] Breen [a representative of the Classis of Holland] read and discussed the high points of the MUTUAL AGREEMENT FOR SEPARATION. A motion was made and seconded that the document with initialed changes be signed and executed tonight. Motion carried."

A letter to the congregation, dated January 31, 1990, included the following statements: "Through serious and frank discussions that took place during the month of January, both the pastors and elders identified long-term concerns and issues. Attempting to follow the Biblical injunction recorded in Matt. 18.15-17, both parties sought counsel from the Classis [of Holland]. Further conversations identified irreconcilable differences. The pastor was encouraged to seek relocation but was not asked to resign. The pastor, however, chose to submit his resignation. This was followed by a period of negotiations with Classis, Consistory, and the pastor. A mutual agreement was signed on January 30, 1990...."

The letter was signed by Pastor Roorda, Beth E. Marcus, vice-president of the consistory, the Rev. Larry Schuyler, chairperson of the Pastoral Supervision and Church Relations Committee of the Classis of Holland, and Delores Bechtel, clerk of the consistory. Pastor Roorda, in the separation agreement, received full salary and benefits until March 31, 1991. He went on staff of the Preston Hollow Presbyterian Church in Dallas, Texas, a congregation of 3,500 members, on April 1, 1991.

41. Conversation with Erma Bruggink, May 12, 1994.
42. A description of the program appeared in *The Church Herald*, June 3, 1988. The author was Kenneth Bradsell. Another view of the origins of the program is in "A Child Shall Lead Them: Reflections on a Decade of Worshiping with Children," by Collette Volkema DeNooyer, in *Reformed Review*, Winter, 1994-95, vol. 48, no. 2, pp. 108-121.
43. *Bulletin* insert, September 6, 1987; *The Third Generation*, September, 1988, p. 8.
44. Hope Reformed, 1984; Iglesia Hispana, 1986; Fourteenth Street Christian Reformed, 1988; and Maple Ave. Christian Reformed, n.d.
45. Information supplied by Elly Muiderman.
46. *The Third Generation*, June, 1981, page 7.
47. *The Third Generation*, April, 1986, p. 19.

48. MasterPlan, Draft 5/4/1992, p. 5.
49. Dennis Voskuil.
50. Dale Van Lente.
51. There is considerable literature on this theme. The principal sources used were the essays, "American Identity and Americanization," by Philip Gleason, pp. 31-58; and "Assimilation and Pluralism," by Harold J. Abramson, pp. 150-160, *The Harvard Encyclopedia of American Ethnic Groups*, 1980.
52. *Webster's New World Dictionary of American English*, Third College Edition, 1988, p. 44.
53. "The Transition Period," in the anniversary booklet, Third Reformed Church, Holland, Michigan. *Historical Celebration Souvenir of the Fiftieth Year of Its Organization, September Nine, Nineteen Hundred Seventeen, 1867-1917*, pp. 16-17.
54. *The Rise of the Unmeltable Ethnics: Politics and Culture in the Seventies*, New York, 1971. See also "Return to the Melting Pot: Ethnicity in the United States in the Eighties," by Rudolph J. Vecoli, in the *Journal of American Ethnic History*, vol. 5, no. 1, Fall, 1985, pp. 7-20 for a discussion of this idea.
55. Dr. Donald A. Luidens, a professor of sociology at Hope College, confirmed the author's thesis on this subject in a conversation with the author Thursday, August 20, 1992. In a statement printed in the Appendix of the MasterPlan, it is claimed that while Third now bridges the upper middle class and the lower upper class, Holland itself is increasingly a blue collar town due to the establishment of several successful manufacturing firms such as the Haworth Company, the Herman Miller Company, and the Prince Corporation, which employ many thousands of workers. Dr. Luidens brought this matter to the attention of the Master Planning Committee.
56. It had been noted in chapter four that Gerrit J. Kollen, Henry Boers, John H. Kleinheksel, and Arend Visscher supported a catechist, Elijah Chinnappa, in India. These young men, graduates of Hope College, had significant careers. Sons of Dutch immigrants, Kollen, Boers, and Kleinheksel were appointed to the Hope College faculty in 1878, the year they banded together to support Chinnappa. Visscher, the sole Hope graduate in 1872, was a Holland attorney. Visscher succeeded Isaac Cappon as Third's Sunday school superintendent in 1890. Gerrit

J. Kollen was president of Hope College, 1893-1911. *Hope College Anniversary Directory*, 1951. Marian Anderson Stryker, editor, p. 215.

57. "Third Church: Fifty Years of Change, 1942-92," presented as a mini-course on the subject of the history of Third Church on October 25, 1992. On file in the archives of the church.

58. See the full text of Dr. Stam's sermon in Appendix 21.

Index